WORDS
OF LIFE

A 1-Year Weekly Devotional

Presented by R. S. Dugan

WORDS OF LIFE : A 1-YEAR WEEKLY DEVOTIONAL
Copyright © 2023 by Spirit & Truth

All rights reserved. Printed in the United States of America. No part of this book may be used or reproduced in any manner whatsoever without written permission except in the case of brief quotations em- bodied in critical articles or reviews.

For information contact :
SPIRIT & TRUTH
PO BOX 1737
MARTINSVILLE, IN 46151
spiritandtruthonline.org

Book and Cover design by
ISBN:

First Edition: December 2023

10 9 8 7 6 5 4 3 2 1

INTRODUCTION
by R. S. Dugan

As an author, words mean the world to me.

It seems like such an incredibly long time ago that God placed the desire on my heart to delve deeper into certain words in Scripture. Yet, on the other hand, this important aspect of my spiritual walk grew much clearer when I became a mom.

My son was a little bit of a late talker; by 18 months, he was still mostly syllabic in his communication, though he had certain words with multitudinous meanings. For a while there, "button" and "bah" were his favorite words, and they encompassed a number of things: light switches, water bottles, his uncle, certain toys, books...and very seldom actual *buttons*.

Yet as I walked through that season of life with him, I became keenly aware of how crucial words are to how we understand and interact with the world around us. The more words he gained and the more articulate he became, the better I was able to understand his heart and intentions.

I will never forget when he began to say "I love you", once he began to grasp the *concept* of love. It's one thing to hear a word or phrase echoed; another to hear it spoken with meaning. And it entirely alters our relationship with someone when we can communicate with them in such a way that their words—whether spoken, written, signed, etc.—and the intentions they convey, are clearly understood.

Most of us don't vividly remember a time before we had the words to communicate our needs, feelings, and desires. Words become second nature to us as our vocabularies expand with time and age, and we can lose sight of the depthless importance of words...all of the things they convey and what they make possible for us.

Yet God is not imprecise with *His* words. Language has long been a tool by which mankind has communicated with one another...but we can't afford to lose sight of the fact that God also uses words to elucidate and instruct us in spiritual realities, holy conduct, and so much more.

As we read the Bible more and more, the words and concepts can become just that to us...words on a page. Esoteric ideas. We can tend to take them for granted, gloss over them, and overlook the importance of why God chooses certain words or concepts to make His truth known.

The aim of this devotional is to slow down. To pause and linger over words in Scripture and the concepts they evoke. To invite you to ponder, "Why *that* word?"

What does it truly mean that something is a "fruit" of the "spirit"? What is it to be in "relationship" with God? Is "destiny" a biblical concept? Is "modesty" all about clothing? Is "sobriety" simply a matter of limiting or avoiding substances?

All of these kinds of questions drew me deeper into this search for the truth behind the words God uses to teach and train us in His ways. And I hope this devotional helps you to gain a broader understanding and greater appreciation for, not just God's Word, but His *words*.

After all...words can be a source of life. Let's learn them and speak them well.

God bless you!
R. S. Dugan

SPIRIT AND TRUTH

SPIRIT

WHEN I WAS A KID, sometimes I doubted whether I had holy spirit. That's typical, I guess, when you're raised around a spiritual concept and you finally hit that age where you start trying to grasp the esoteric implications of it. It just didn't connect with me for a long time what holy spirit *was* or how it *worked,* or whether it was even present in me. That doubt persisted into my teen years.

One day, I was watching a TV show with my dad where a character spoke of his "gut feeling"—almost a joke among the cast, although that gut feeling was very rarely wrong. Utterly unprompted, my dad turned to me and said, "That's what the holy spirit feels like sometimes, you know? Like a gut feeling."

And it clicked. My whole life, I had been feeling the presence and power exerted by the gift of holy spirit I received when I made Christ my Lord, so long ago I don't even remember it. I just never knew that's what it was.

Once I connected with that feeling, there was no holding back. It was time to move beyond simple gut nudges and start manifesting that spirit's power in my life, like Jesus did when he walked the earth two thousand years ago.

What is Spirit?

In this context, **spirit** refers to the gift of holy spirit that is instilled in each Christian when they accept Jesus as their savior. It differs from *the Holy Spirit*, a name for one of the attributes of God, in that it isn't a being, but a supernatural force. The source texts from which Scripture is translated use the same word for this power as they do for things like "breath" or "wind," because it's that same kind of invisible power that you can't see, but you can *feel* its presence.

So what is this spirit, exactly? It's a portion of God's essence inside us! God is holy and He is a spirit-being, so His power is holy spirit. Having holy spirit within us allows us to manifest the power of God in everyday situations, just like Jesus, Peter, Paul, Moses, Aaron, and others did. These people all did those great miracles, signs, and wonders and taught powerful things through communion with God via the gift of holy spirit.

What Does the Bible Say About the Gift of Holy Spirit?

1 Corinthians 6:19 - Or do you not know that your body is a sanctuary of the **holy spirit** that is in you, which you have from God, and you are not your own?

Acts 2:4 - And they were all filled with **holy spirit**, and began to speak in other tongues, as the Spirit was giving to them utterance.

2 Timothy 1:14 - The good deposit that was committed *to you*, guard through **holy spirit** that dwells in us.

HOW DO I KNOW THAT I HAVE THE GIFT OF HOLY SPIRIT?

If you are a born-again Christian, you have been sealed with holy spirit. There's no doubt about that! Every Christian receives this gift when they accept Christ as their savior. But there are lots of ways to become more aware of its presence.

One of these ways is by what Scripture calls "manifestations". These include speaking in tongues, prophecy, miracles, and revelation, among others, and each one is a way the holy spirit within us *manifests* in the temporal realm for the good of us and those around us.

Another is by the fruit we bear in our lives—qualities that God refers to as "the fruit of the spirit." The more we walk by the power of the spirit within us, the more we will exemplify these attributes of God's nature, which honors Him tremendously!

Another example of holy spirit within us that some Christians don't always recognize as such is that they'll feel a great discomfort about doing things that are contrary to the will of God. This is one of the many ways that the holy spirit is a "helper" to us; it kind of acts like a Jiminy Cricket on our shoulder, a conscience that pings us when we're behaving or engaging in things that go against God's desires.

TAKE ACTION:

Take some time this week to read Galatians 5 and 1 Corinthians 12 in depth. Learn and study the gift of holy spirit. Then search for ways to walk more by the spirit in your day-to-day life!

FRUIT

HAVE YOU EVER BEEN IN a mood so rotten you felt like you reeked?

I think if we're being honest, we've all been there. Sometimes we get so fed up that something spews out of our mouth that makes us go, "Wow, even I know that was savage!" At that moment, the odiousness of our bad mood becomes something everyone else can smell, reeking like rotten fruit.

Everyone bears fruit with their actions. We're all basically fleshy little trees with hobbies. The older I get, the more mindful I become of the fruit I'm bearing and how it reflects, not only on my whole person, but on the One I represent. When I choose to dwell on the blessings of life, I like to think I'm pretty sunshiny to be around. But people take notice when I'm stuck in the negative, too.

If only we could stop growing fruit when we're in the low points and only be known for what we produce in the peaks of life! But it doesn't work that way. We're always bearing fruit. The question is, what kind?

It can be easy to look at lists in the Bible, like the fruit of the spirit in Galatians 5 or the "love list" in 1 Corinthians 13, and think that if we *do those things*, then we will spiritually sound. But we've actually got it backward!

When we are living by the spirit, we produce the fruit of the spirit naturally; and when we walk in love, we naturally show the attributes listed in 1 Corinthians 13. We should always bear in mind that the Christian walk doesn't come with a checkbox of tasks that we must complete in order to become holy or good; instead, God gives us instructions for powerful spiritual principles which, if we live by them, will produce good fruit in us.

WHAT IS FRUIT?

Merriam-Webster Dictionary defines **fruit** (in this context) as "the effect or consequence of an action or operation."

The Bible speaks often of fruit—the fruits of labor, the fruits of harvest, and the fruit we are to bear as followers of Jesus Christ. Historically, people brought sacrifices to God from the firstfruits of their harvest and herds. Jesus is called the firstfruits from among the dead (meaning the first person raised from death to everlasting life).

Ultimately, everyone on earth produces fruit by their words and deeds, either good or bad...a harvest that comes directly from what they're made up of on the inside. In nature, everything comes after its own kind—apples from apple trees, pears from pear trees, and so forth—and the same is true in the spiritual sense. So it's up to every individual to make sure they are producing good fruit in their lives to the praise of God's glory.

WHAT DOES THE BIBLE SAY ABOUT FRUIT?

Matthew 7:15-20 - "Beware of the false prophets, who come to you in sheep's clothing, but inwardly are ravenous wolves. "**You will know them by their fruits.** Grapes are not gathered from thorn bushes nor figs from thistles, are they?" So every good tree bears good fruit, but the bad tree bears bad fruit.

Philippians 1:9-11 - And this I pray, that your love may abound still more and more in real knowledge and all discernment, so that you may approve the things that are excellent, in order to be sincere and blameless until the day of Christ; having been filled with **the fruit of righteousness** which comes through Jesus Christ, to the glory and praise of God.

Luke 8:15 - But the seed in the good soil, these are the ones who have heard the word in an honest and good heart, and hold it fast, **and bear fruit with perseverance.**

HOW CAN I BEAR GOOD FRUIT?

One of the beautiful things about Jesus' statement that a good tree bears good fruit, and a bad tree bears bad fruit, is that it makes it easy to gauge the trajectory we're on. If we want to bear good fruit, we need to be walking in the power of holy spirit, which bears the wonderful fruit of love—as well as joy, peace, patience, and more.

One thing we also have to be mindful of when it comes to bearing good fruit is that we can't "fake it to make it" with God. We don't prove we're bearing good fruit by trying to make it seem like we're so holy and so pure, when we've really got rottenness festering on the inside.

God isn't taken in by shiny apples with moldy cores. To bear good fruit, we have to let go of things that lead to rot—resentment, vengeance, addiction, unforgiveness, anger, gossip, jealousy, spite, hatred, etc. In place of these things, which can poison our harvest and cause us to lash out in *unfruitful* ways, we have to let the holy spirit power of God transform us from the inside out. It's the only way to truly produce a good harvest in our thoughts and actions.

We can pretend to be holy all we like—and sadly Christianity has developed a reputation of doing just that!—but Jesus tells us that essentially, "the fruit will out."

In order to truly bear good fruit, we have to do the hard work to become good trees watered in the life-giving water poured out by our Savior, Jesus.

TAKE ACTION:

Take time to assess the fruit your life is bearing. Is it good or bad? What can you do to continuously improve your harvest?

LOVE

I HEARD SOMEONE SAY ONCE that love is a unifying language. I have had friends through the years with whom it was often difficult to communicate for one reason or another, yet a loving act done by one of us for the other never went misunderstood.

Love manifests itself in a lot of ways. My husband shows his love for me by keeping a clean house and changing most of our son's poopy diapers. I try my best to show love in turn by cooking tasty, healthy meals and keeping our boy happy and healthy. Love can often look like compassion or correction, like giving or lending a helping hand. Each one rings differently and each is profound.

Jesus told us that love would prove to people who we are—his disciples. For love, God sent His Son to die for us, and for love, Jesus went. You do not need to speak the same tongue to speak the language of love to someone.

During a car ride one day, my brother and I got deep into discussing how to reach people with the message of Christ. Where we landed after nearly an hour of back-and-forth on such controversial topics as sexuality, addiction, and other sins was this: If you don't lead with unbiased, sincere, from-the-heart love, you're leading with the wrong foot.

Life is a dance. Love is the music that guides us in perfect rhythm to the steps of God. After all, if we don't have love...what are we doing but making noise?

WHAT IS LOVE?

Merriam-Webster Dictionary defines love as "a feeling of strong or constant affection for a person."

In the Greek language from which the New Testament and Septuagint (Greek Old Testament) are translated, there are several different words for love, and four widely-known: **agapē** (related to obedience and commitment, not necessarily feeling and emotion), **eros** (romantic or sexual affection, appears only in Septuagint), **phileō** (implies a strong emotional connection, and thus is used of the deep love between friends), and **storgē** (naturally occurs between parents and children, can exist between siblings, and exists between husbands and wives in a good marriage).

Each kind of love has a different application in Scripture, and it's important that we know which love we are called to show and toward whom, so that we can be confident we are walking in the love to which we are.

What Does the Bible Say About Love?

John 3:16: For God so loved (**agapē**) the world that he gave his only begotten Son, so that whoever believes in him will not perish, but have life in the age to come.

John 21:15: Jesus: Simon...do you love (*agapē*) me more than these [fish?]. Peter: Yes, Lord; you know that I love (*phileō*) you.

Romans 12:10: As to brotherly affection—*have* family affection (*storgē)* toward one another.

Proverbs 7:18: Come, let us drink our fill of lovemaking until the morning; let us delight ourselves with much love (*eros*).

How Can I Become More Loving?

Because the nature of God is love, the more we behave like Him and follow His instructions for right and righteous living, the more loving we will be. This process is often referred to as "putting off the old man nature" and "putting on the new man"—that is, the nature of God. Ephesians 4 gives us a list of just a few things in this "put off, put on" process that we can do to be more like God, which by default will make us more loving in our interactions with everyone:

- Put away falsehood and speak the truth to each other.
- Even when you're angry, don't sin and don't give opportunity to the Devil.
- Don't steal.

- Let no corrupting talk proceed out of your mouth, but only what is good for edifying according to the need, so that it gives grace to those who hear.
- Do not grieve the holy spirit of God with which you were sealed until the day of redemption.
- Get rid of all bitterness and rage and anger and angry shouting and defaming speech, along with all malice.
- Be kind to one another, tenderhearted.
- Forgive each other, just as God also has forgiven you in Christ.

There are many other things we can do to become more loving people overall, including: being more focused on others than ourselves, training our hearts to be thankful at all times, listening empathically, giving when able, and more.

Ultimately, loving behavior comes both from feeling (***eros, phileō, storgē***) and action (***agapē***), and we must dedicate our hearts to learning, understanding, and walking out each kind of love that God calls us into.

WORDS OF LIFE

TAKE ACTION:

What is one thing from the list in Ephesians 4 that you can focus on this week that will help you be more loving?

JOY

THERE ARE MOMENTS OF JOY that stay with you. I remember being eight years old the winter I got my first dog, the first time I remember experiencing what I would call *joy*. After years and years of tearful pleading, my parents finally adopted Harley Davidson, my Christmas present that year, about three weeks before the actual holiday. I spent every waking moment with him, but one in particular sticks out.

It was nighttime—late, it felt like, but probably just because it was winter. Harley and I ran ourselves ragged playing steal-the-mitten in the backyard, and I finally flopped down flat on my back on the frigid ground. Harley climbed onto my chest—all twenty pounds of supposed-to-be-a-beagle-but-was-actually-a-foxhound—and we lay there quietly. I can still see how the snowfall looked through the industrial lights of the Walgreens building next door. I can still feel his weight on my chest. And I can still remember feeling, in that moment, utter joy.

Not just because I finally had my puppy I'd been begging for. It was everything: the Christmas season, the quiet of the snow, the fact that my parents showed their love by opening their home to a dog I wanted so badly. The love of the dog on my chest. The love of God I felt that night, like He was smiling down at me, and the way I reflected that love back to Harley. At eight years old, watching the snow fall from the dark sky, for the first time I truly conceptualized two things: the peace of God and the joy it brought.

Even now, the memory brings tears to my eyes. Because in that moment, I felt joy in the security of

God's love and the love of my family in a truly tangible way. And it is a feeling I will never forget, because it was then I first experienced the difference between happiness and joy.

Happiness was having my puppy. Joy was in that moment, fathoming the love of my family and my God.

WHAT IS JOY?

Merriam-Webster Dictionary defines **joy** as "the emotion evoked by well-being, success, or good fortune, or by the prospect of possessing what one desires."

Many people equate joy with happiness, but biblically these are separate concepts. Happiness is circumstantial—we are usually happy when things go well for us. Joy, on the other hand, scripturally speaking, is a sense of well-being reliant on trust in God, regardless of our present circumstances. Happiness is fleeting; joy is eternal.

WHAT DOES THE BIBLE SAY ABOUT JOY?

Hebrews 10:34 - For you had compassion on those in prison, and **joyfully** accepted the seizure of your property, knowing that you have for yourselves a better possession, and a lasting *one*.

James 1:2-3 - My brothers *and sisters*, count it all **joy** when you fall into various temptations, knowing that the testing of your trust produces endurance.

1 Peter 1:8 - Though you have not seen [Jesus Christ], you love him, and though you do not see him now, but believe in him, you rejoice greatly with inexpressible and glorious **joy**,

How Can I Become More Joyful?

The key to joyfulness is to be firmly grounded in the promises and hope from God, recognizing that the commission He has given us and the rewards He promises far exceed the temporal happiness that can be found by pursuing the pleasures of this life. Indeed, the second fruit of the spirit—the list of attributes that manifest from walking by the gift of God's holy spirit in us—is joy! Thus, when we are focused on the things of the spirit rather than of the flesh, we become more joyful.

For some, it takes coming face-to-face with the fragility of this life and its fleeting offerings to truly grasp and embrace joy eternal. Nevertheless, our goal should *always* be to increase in joy by deepening our understanding and thankfulness for all God has done and will do for us, and also to nurture a deeper appreciation and excitement for what is yet to come.

The better we understand God's promises and the hope of our guaranteed future, the easier it is to be joyful in any circumstances, like the writer of Hebrews 10 spoke of. Despite having their possessions seized, the followers of Jesus **joyfully accepted** the circumstance, knowing there was something far greater in store for them. They may not have been *happy* about what happened, but they remained *joyful* because they knew their well-being was in God's hands and that loss of possessions in this life did not touch the promise of possessing what they truly desired in the age to come.

Similarly, in the book of Philippians Paul set a wonderful example for living joyfully regardless of circumstances—penning a letter with pure joy as a theme while he was in prison! Many great men and women of the faith lived lives that were great proof of the grounding, stabilizing aspect of joy: that it is not based on how great things are going for us, but instead in how great a God we serve!

TAKE ACTION:

In your life, do you tend to pursue happiness, or joy? In what way could you shift your behavior or perspective to live more fully in the joy of the Lord?

PEACE

PEACE CAN BE HARD-WON in this day and age. Yet that abundant, deep peace is something God wants for each of us. Something He is willing to lead us into. Something everyone can have if they're willing to put forth the time and effort and set up the boundaries that invite peace rather than stress into their lives.

I spent years learning methods of God-focused meditation to combat my anxiety—ways of tackling problem areas, particularly obsessive recurring thoughts, by leading them captive to Christ and submersing them in peace. For me, this peace comes from slowing down, reciting Scripture, dwelling on positive experiences, and then slowly going back to tackle the thought with my hand firmly in God's.

If you struggle with being peaceful, know that you are not alone. This is not abnormal, even among Christians. There are different ways of achieving peace, and I hope this will help you on the road to finding the way that works for you.

What is Peace?

Merriam-Webster Dictionary defines **peace** as "freedom from disquieting or oppressive thoughts or emotions." There is also the peace that is a state of tranquility within a person, or of harmony or mutual concord between different factions.

The Bible speaks of different kinds of peace and the different ways we achieve them. A peaceful and peaceable life is something God desires for all mankind, and it is something most people strive for in numerous ways—from healthy ones like ridding ourselves of toxic influences and living a life of gratitude, to unhealthy ones like conflict avoidance or even by oppression or control of dissenting points of view.

But ultimate tranquility, concordance, and freedom from disquieting or oppressive thoughts or emotions can only be attained through relationship with Jesus Christ.

WHAT DOES THE BIBLE SAY ABOUT PEACE?

Colossians 3:15 - Let the **peace of Christ** rule in your hearts, since as members of one body you were called to **peace**. And be thankful.

Hebrews 12:14 - Make every effort to **live in peace** with everyone and to be holy; without holiness no one will see the Lord.

Philippians 4:7 - And the **peace of God**, which transcends all understanding, will guard your hearts and your minds in Christ Jesus.

Psalms 29:11 - The LORD gives strength to his people; **the LORD blesses his people with peace.**

How Can I Be More Peaceful?

Scripture makes it clear on many occasions that having simple human "peace" is not enough to lift the burden of trouble from our lives. We need a heavenly peace that passes understanding in order to experience true soul-rest in contentment and security regardless of life's shortcomings.

Before Jesus ascended to the Father's right hand, one of the last things he gave his followers was *peace*. In fact, he emphasized that he was leaving *his* peace with them, and not the kind the world gives (John 14:27). Specifically through our union with Christ, we will have peace that passes understanding (Phil. 4:7). When the Book of Isaiah listed the attributes of the then-future Messiah, one of them was that he would be the *prince of peace* (Isaiah 9:6). The braiding together of perfect peace and the presence of Christ has quite literally been a highlight of his very existence since the angel first announced his birth to the shepherds in Luke 2!

This aspect of Jesus' purpose and character is driven home again in Ephesians 2, where emphasis is placed on Jesus Christ as our peace. The sense of unity in the spirit and peace among Christians comes through Jesus and not by our *own* sense of things. We are incapable of experiencing true peace personally or *inter*personally if it does not come through

Christ—his teachings, his dealings, and how he works with us all.

Jesus brought a new sense of peace to the world. He died on the cross, opening a path to perfect peace in union with him, and through him, with the Father. He also encourages his followers to live peaceably among others as much as they can, even going so far as to love their enemies and pray for those who persecute them! Even in times of distress, doubt, persecution and struggle, we can still be peaceful when our trust is firmly placed in Christ and in God.

So when you're feeling troubled, ask yourself whose peace you're relying on: your own, or the peace of Christ? Are you upholding him as your peace, or striving for a personal sense of solace and unity that comes through the human perspective— the peace the world tries to offer?

Jesus gave us many examples in his teachings of how to live peaceably with one another despite our differences, as well as with those currently outside the Body of Christ. He also speaks with us through the holy spirit dwelling in us. He can and *will* show you the path to peace through him—who is himself our *peace*.

TAKE ACTION:

What is an area of your life where you could use more peace? Lift it up in prayer to Jesus today and trust in him to help you find a way through, as he has promised!

PATIENCE

ANOTHER SLAM. ANOTHER CRASH. ANOTHER "UH-OH."

Those who have parented a child through toddlerhood, as I have, likely recognize this chorus all too well. In our household, it was often a daily occurrence with a 2-year-old: the reminders to use soft hands on the kitties, to not throw heavy wooden hand-carved trains, to stop competing for most number of strawberry slices or Puffs shoved into the mouth all at once.

The good news I have for you is this: the twos are not actually as terrible as people forewarn. The bad news—or what I like to call the "learning opportunity"—is that you will likely be repeating the same instructions over and over and over and OVER again, waiting for it to finally take root in that little mind that is still developing consideration over impulse control.

Oh, what golden opportunities for patience. It's so easy to default to frustration when a toddler does something that *we* know better about—like smacking his sleeping cat on the ribs—and my own impulse in these circumstances is often a harsh scolding, or even to lose my temper.

Yet over and over God has beckoned me back to His quiet place, reminding me to be patient and calm. Reminding me that I was—and am—training a developing mind. One that does not have the wisdom of experience or foresight that I do as an adult.

Patience, I have so many times felt God calling to me. Patience with a little boy who is learning how to be a person Who is compelled by impulse and has not yet developed a capacity for wisdom and foresight. Patience when I tell him to do this or that, and he doesn't; or when I tell him not to do something, and he does it anyway.

Parenthood has given me such a unique perspective on how endless and abiding God's patience must be, when He has millions and millions of kids who are all just like my boy. And who are so fiercely loved, just as he is—and we are loved perfectly by a patient God who knows how we struggle with our impulses, and stumble, and still try so hard to please Him.

What lessons we can learn from the patience of our Heavenly Father!

WHAT IS PATIENCE?

Merriam-Webster Dictionary defines **patience** as "the capacity, habit, or fact of being patient; bearing pains or trials calmly or without complaint; manifesting forbearance under provocation or strain."

Patience is something every Christian needs, because we will spend a lot of our lives waiting for things promised in the future—like godly justice, perfect bodies, everlasting life, and the return of Christ. We also need a lot of that forbearance, which is "a refraining from the enforcement of something (such as a debt, right, or obligation) that is due," because it's not our place to enforce these things in many cases...it's God's job to dole out righteous judgement.

Patience also helps us bear up under mistreatment, which Jesus warns that every Christian will face at one point or another. Having a patient attitude helps us not to become overwhelmed or anxious for the things of God, but rather to be sound-minded and able to continuously serve Him while we wait.

What Does the Bible Say About Patience?

Ephesians 4:2 - Be always humble, gentle, and **patient**. Show your love by being **tolerant** with one another.

Romans 12:12 - Let your hope keep you joyful, be **patient** in your troubles, and pray at all times.

1 Corinthians 13:4 - Love is **patient** and kind; it is not jealous or conceited or proud...

How Can I Become More Patient?

Because it is a fruit of our spiritual life and thus a reflection of where we're living spiritually, growing our patience can really come from two places: active choice and state of mind. Often we have to actively choose to be patient until it becomes a habitual mindset. To strengthen our patience, we begin by not giving sway to our *im*patient thoughts and actions.

So let's say you're in line at the grocery store and you're tempted to roll your eyes and start muttering under your breath when the person in line ahead of you takes way too long; practice patience right then. Instead of giving in to those urges to vocalize or stew in your impatience, do something beneficial. Don't even give your impatience the time of day! Mentally reshuffle your priorities and do something useful while you wait in line.

The same goes for any situation where your patience is tested. If you're in traffic and it's getting on your last nerve, don't sit and dwell on how annoying that is. Take time to turn up the music or call a friend (and talk about something *besides the traffic)* or PRAY! Or if you're with a group of people who tend to bring out the impatience in you, pause and pray for them rather than airing all your complaints.

Let the holy spirit in you work outward to be other-focused and not all about the things that are making you impatient. When you're walking in the spirit, you'll discover even more ways you can turn a patience-testing situation into one that glorifies the Lord!

TAKE ACTION:

Throughout your week, practice conscious patience in the best and especially the worst situations.

KINDNESS

KINDNESS. SUCH A PRIVILEGE AND a challenge to extend. How easy it is to show kindness to a beloved friend in good times, to a well-behaved pet, to a coworker who's done something solid for you.

How difficult when a friend is trapped in a mess of their own making. When the cat tears the curtains. When a coworker keeps missing deadlines.

I've learned with time that kindness should never depend on how I feel. It doesn't matter if I *feel* like being kind to my cat, I'm still not going to kick her. Nor will I leap down my friend's throat and berate him for the mess he's made. Nor will I go off on a tangent against my coworker and gossip about them behind their back.

When we make kindness our default approach, while it may not fix a bad situation, we are not in a position to make it worse. Kindness—whether gentle or firm—begets far more correction and change than a hot-tempered word. Whether we're comforting a hurt heart, confronting a habitual bad practice, or even meeting someone for the very first time, leading with kindness influences the situation and steers it toward the best possible outcome.

And honestly, we could all use a little more kindness both given and received, couldn't we?

What is Kindness?

Merriam-Webster Dictionary defines **kindness** as "the quality or state of being kind; of a sympathetic or helpful nature; of a forbearing nature."

It seems we can hardly turn left or right these days without encountering someone who's suffered from unkindness, someone who's being unkind, or else we ourselves are facing the temptation to be unkind. But one of the greatest qualities Jesus exuded—and I think one of the qualities that still draws people most strongly to him—was his kindness. He helped those the society of that day turned their backs on: lepers and cripples and tax collectors and sinners. He touched the untouchable, challenged Sabbath laws to heal the needy, and changed countless lives...actions that resonate to this day.

"Random acts of kindness" are considered one of the faith-restoring hallmarks of humanity; deep down, all of us are moved to varying levels when we witness an act of pure kindness done without deceit or self-aggrandization.

When people behave out of kindness, it fills them with joy. When others witness kindness, it gives them hope. And when people receive kindness, it can change their whole world. It's no wonder kindness is a fruit of the spirit that works in us—its benefits are so widespread, it's one of the clearest ways we see God move in this day and age.

WHAT DOES THE BIBLE SAY ABOUT KINDNESS?

Ephesians 4:32 - Be **kind** to one another, tenderhearted, forgiving each other, just as God in Christ also has forgiven you.

Romans 2:4 - Or do you think lightly of the riches of His **kindness** and tolerance and patience, not knowing that **the kindness of God** leads you to repentance?

Micah 6:8 - And what does the LORD require of you but to do justice, **to love kindness**, and to walk humbly with your God?

How Can I Become Kinder?

Like the other fruits of the spirit, kindness is an integral part of our "new man" nature. Thus, the more we build up our spiritual life and the more we walk according to God's instructions and live by His precepts, the kinder we will naturally be.

Because the nature of God is kindness, when we are nearer to Him, we will reflect kindness even more toward others. We can also cultivate kindness in many ways, such as:

- Putting the needs of others before ourselves.
- Giving special thought to those less fortunate.

- Taking time to speak to others and listen empathically.
- Taking care of those in need.
- Confronting issues in a loving and godly manner.
- Reading the Gospels and studying the example of Christ.
- Praying frequently and fervently for others.
- Leading with love rather than hate.
- Seeking the person behind any problem rather than seeing them for their flaws.

There are just a few of the ways we can both show and grow our loving kindness!

TAKE ACTION:

Make an effort this week to look for someone who is especially in need of kindness; then do your best to meet that need!

GOODNESS

"PERFECT'S THE ENEMY OF GOOD ENOUGH."

This is a line they teach us when it comes to novel-writing. Where the effort for perfection will never get all the way off its butt and do something, being good says, "I recognize I will never be the best of the best there ever was. But that won't stop me from doing great things now."

We are never going to be perfect representations of Jesus in this life. We will never have it all together. We will never achieve perfect knowledge or perfect execution of godly principles. We just won't. But we don't have to. What we have to do is *do good*, right now, with what we have.

We have to follow Jesus. Obey Yahweh. Make a difference. Spread truth. Give love and kindness. Show mercy. Walk humbly.

And we must do this all through the context of goodness, understanding that while we may not do everything perfectly, we will still be about our Father's business.

WHAT IS GOODNESS?

Merriam-Webster Dictionary defines **goodness** as "the quality or state of being good; of a favorable character or tendency."

The word used for "goodness" in this context in the Greek language referred to moral uprightness or excellence in one's heart and life. Goodness strives for what is right even if it's not what is easy. It draws distinct moral lines in the sand and adheres to what God qualifies as right, turning away from what He deems wrong. Goodness is a way of being that cares more about being right with God than right with man, no matter the consequences.

What Does the Bible Say About Goodness?

Titus 2:14 – [Jesus] gave himself for us to redeem us from all wickedness and to purify for himself a people that are his very own, eager to do **what is good**.

Psalm 37:3 - Trust in the Lord and **do good**; dwell in the land and enjoy safe pasture.

Matthew 5:16 - In the same way, let your light shine before others, that they may see your **good deeds** and glorify your Father in heaven.

How Can I Increase in Goodness?

Goodness, like the other fruits of the spirit, is a natural outworking of a spirit-driven life. When we become focused on the things of God and make an effort to walk by the spirit, matters of right or wrong become much more black and white. As uncomfortable as this can be, especially living in a world where many issues are blurred in shades of gray, we have a responsibility before God to do our best to walk in moral uprightness in our hearts and lives. So, naturally, we increase in goodness by pursuing the things of God above the things of the world, and also by consciously turning from things that try to pull us away from Him.

Living in goodness requires a level of dying to self so that we can live for God. It's rarely easy, but thankfully the spirit working in us helps lessen the strain. It encourages us in our inner being to reach out for those things of God, and when we feel tempted by the distractions of this life, we may even feel an internal friction that compels us to turn away from those distractions and back into the arms of our Heavenly Father.

Doing good deeds and living in the goodness of the spirit is not a level of spirituality we achieve; it's a lifelong process. Because of our sin nature, we'll always battle against the urge to do what's easy over what's right. Sometimes we'll win, sometimes we'll lose.

But thank God we have that holy spirit in us, that God works in us to want to do and to do His will! This makes it easier to see the profit of denying what tempts us and instead living a life of goodness that is a joy to God, a wonderful witness of Him and His Son, and a blessing to those we encounter.

TAKE ACTION:

Make it a point this week to put the things of God before the distractions of this life and do good above all else!

FAITHFULNESS

IF YOU WANT A QUICK AND crucial lesson on living faithfully, marriage is the life for you.

One thing I've learned, sometimes painfully, within my marriage is that faithfulness to my husband is a lot more than just not cheating. It's about putting his needs first, above my own or anyone else's; being in a partnership with him where

I don't just do my own thing, I am in conversation with him about life and the things that matter; I am loyal to him, which means not just wanting him and him alone, but also respecting his boundaries, keeping his confidences, defending, encouraging, and loving him; and also remaining faithful to him, and him alone, for as long as we both live.

I don't think it's any coincidence that the relationship between Jesus and the Church is likened to a husband and bride. For our part as the Body, the "bride," there is an element of faithfulness required of us in this relationship with our savior. It's the faithfulness I've grown familiar with through years of marriage. And the more I learn about faithfulness, the more I have to ask myself...

Am I putting Jesus above myself? Am I in partnership with him where I don't just do my own thing? Am I loyal to him, respectful of him? Have I kept my vow from when I made him my Lord, to remain steadfast even when other things seek my attention, my loyalty, my love?

Am I living faithfully for my Lord?

What is Faithfulness?

Merriam-Webster Dictionary defines **faithfulness** as "steadfast in affection or allegiance; firm in adherence to promises or in observance of duty."

Faithfulness is an intrinsic part of the Christian life. We should always strive to be faithful to our partners, spouses, and faithful in our words and deeds. We are also called to allegiance to God, which means that we are devoted and loyal to Him, and only Him—placing no other god, no superstition, no person or thing, no idol or object, on the throne of our heart where He belongs.

Allegiance is used often in terms of vassals and liege lords, where the loyalty of the subject to their lord was absolute, and that's definitely an aspect of our relationship with God. In the angle of adherence and duty, our faithfulness requires that we're about our Father's business, doing the work of God as we have been commissioned and called by Him and by Jesus.

Likewise, as we are called to be faithful to God, the Bible shows us in many places that He is faithful toward us, such as how He keeps His promises and is steadfast in His affection. He also takes his fatherly role with us very seriously, ensuring our wellbeing in all things.

What Does the Bible Say About Faithfulness?

1 John 1:9 - If we confess our sins, **he is faithful** and just to forgive us our sins and to cleanse us from all unrighteousness.

Lamentations 3:23 – [Your mercies] are new every morning; **great is your faithfulness**.

Deuteronomy 32:4 - The Rock, his work is perfect, for all his ways are justice. **A God of faithfulness** and without iniquity, just and upright is he.

How Can I Become More Faithful?

Just like the other fruits of the spirit, we become more faithful to God as we walk by the spirit, learning and growing in our relationship with Him. The closer we become to God and the more we prioritize and focus on the things that are important to Him, the more it will engender that steadfastness of our affection for Him that is a key factor of faithfulness.

As for the allegiance side of faithfulness, that will become natural as we walk in the spirit as well. But it is also something we pledge to in our hearts and lives on a daily basis. Our allegiance to God means that He comes first, before anything else we may do or want to do; it means we must choose God moment by moment, hour by hour, day by day, consecrating our hearts to Him over and over for His purpose and will.

We become more faithful when we put God first, observe our duties to Him, and walk more and more in the spirit that lives within us, which binds us closely to Him.

TAKE ACTION:

Do you feel like you're being faithful to God before all else? If not, how can you adjust your priorities to place Him on the throne of your heart where He deserves to be?

MEEKNESS

WHAT'S YOUR DEFAULT POSITION WHEN someone confronts you with a mistake you made or a way you showed up that was less than beneficial to those around you?

If you find you default to defensiveness, irritation, anger, and the like, then you're not alone. This is where we must pivot to a position of *meekness*.

Meekness is a struggle for a lot of people because in their minds, it's translated to weakness...but in fact, meekness requires a tremendous amount of strength and solid character to live out.

It's meekness, not haughtiness, that heads off a fight. Being willing to submit to godly correction is a mark of spiritual maturity, not a flaw. And it's actually meekness that allows us to grow in understanding, wisdom, and overall spiritual strength, because the meek are open to seeing places where they can improve and accepting advice that will help them get there.

It is meekness that allows us to see our broken, sinful state and accept the only healing for these things: the saving grace of Jesus.

And that is why it's the meek, those willing to come face-to-face with their flaws and accept the help of the Savior, that will inherit the future earth.

What is Meekness?

Merriam-Webster Dictionary defines **meekness** or **gentleness** as "the quality or state of being gentle, especially mildness of manners or disposition."

Meekness involves a submissive attitude to God with the willingness to be reproved and correct our course as needed. It is that temper of spirit in which we accept His dealings with us as good, and therefore without resisting.

It must be clearly understood that godly meekness is a mental posture of power, not weakness. The common assumption is that meekness is synonymous with "mousy" or "cowardly," but Jesus was "meek" because he had the infinite resources of God at his command. Someone who is meek can afford to be so because his strength and confidence allows him to listen well to others. Moses was the meekest man on earth at his time, but his was a walk of powerful signs and wonders.

Meekness is a way of being, opposed to boldness or brashness of manner; it's expected as the default behavior for leaders in the Body of Christ and will be an outworking in us as we walk by the spirit.

What Does the Bible Say About Meekness?

Titus 3:2 - To defame no one, not to be quarrelsome, to be reasonable, showing all **meekness** toward all people...

Galatians 6:1 - Brothers, if anyone is caught in any transgression, you who are spiritual should restore him in a spirit of **meekness**. Keep watch on yourself, lest you too be tempted.

Ephesians 4:2 - With all humility and **meekness**, with patience, bearing with one another in love...

How Can I Become Meeker?

The depths of submission in true meekness stems from spirit-led surrender to God. Like the other fruits of the spirit, it's not something we can fake until we make it. While we can behave meekly, the strength and confidence needed to walk out this sort of strong gentleness before God and with others comes from truly growing in our understanding of God, of our identity in Christ, and walking in the power of the holy spirit as fellow laborers with them.

The beauty of meekness is that it's birthed in the security of knowing who we are and where we stand with God, and through His eyes, seeing the nature of things around us.

Through meekness, we restore people from transgression. Through it, leaders make themselves approachable, showing the appeal of Christ to the wary and skeptical. And through it, we show people the gentle yet unyielding nature of Christ, wherein we are neither shaken by strong winds nor eroded by the weight of our own ego.

TAKE ACTION:

Are there areas of your life where you rely on your perception of strength rather than on meekness before the Lord? Take time in prayer and ask the Lord to help you shift your perspective through the power of the spirit working in you.

SELF-CONTROL

I DON'T THINK IT'S ANY coincidence that self-control is the last fruit of the spirit listed in Galatians 5:23, for the simple fact that in order to bear good fruit, we need to be rooted, grounded, and growing in good things—in "good spirit" that helps produce those fruits.

And in order to pursue godly things, we have to have the self-control to deny ourselves the things that produce bad fruit in our lives.

It's almost cyclical, in a way. Self-control is a fruit of the spirit that empowers us to have better control, so we produce better fruit!

Think about it like this: if you decide to eat healthy, change doesn't just happen overnight. Especially if you're used to eating a lot of junk, you have to first practice self-control before you see results—you have to say no to unhealthy foods and deny the things your body tells you that you *absolutely need right now*. But if you give it enough time, eventually the cravings lessen. This makes it easier to say no to them. Thus, the self-control you exert at the beginning empowers the self-control you need to continue down the road you started on.

But a lot of times, our self-control isn't strong enough to stand on its own. It needs support from Someone much stronger than us! Thankfully, God is there to help us when we're tempted to do things that are harmful to us or detrimental to our growth. He is able and willing to answer prayers for help with controlling our minds, hearts, and actions; and this helps us perpetuate the cycle of denying ourselves and dying to our sinful nature so we can better live lives that please and glorify the Lord.

WHAT IS SELF-CONTROL?

Merriam-Webster Dictionary defines **self-control** as "restraint exercised over one's own impulses, emotions, or desires." Having control over one's instinctive nature is one of the fundamental necessities to living a godly life.

When we confess Jesus as our Lord and his blood covers our sins, we receive holy spirit, which helps transform us into the image of God, who is *the* Holy Spirit.

The Bible calls this new image or new nature the "new man," and the nature of sinfulness devoid of Christ the "old man."

The struggle we face is that while the Holy Spirit helps us and spurs us on to love and good works, the sinful nature that was our former condition does not go down without a fight, so we often face temptations to backslide into harmful practices and bad habits, poor ways of thinking and behavior, etc. This is where we need self-control—to say yes to the good and no to the bad that are at war within us.

WHAT DOES THE BIBLE SAY ABOUT SELF-CONTROL?

1 Peter 1:5-6 - Now for this very reason, make every effort to add to your trust, virtue; and to virtue, knowledge; and to knowledge, **self-control**; and to **self-control**, endurance; and to endurance, godliness...

2 Timothy 1:7 - For God did not give us a spirit of timidity, but of power and love and **self-control**.

Titus 1:8 – [The overseer must be] given to hospitality, liking *what is* good, sensible, righteous, pure, **self-controlled**...

How Can I Become More Self-Controlled?

There are two aspects to self-control. Thankfully, the working of God's holy spirit in us helps with both! While we will always have that struggle between our old and new natures, the "helper" Jesus sent through the gift of holy spirit gives us a kind of spiritual "boost" where we feel the pressure in our spirits to want to do, and to do, what pleases God. While we still have the free will to choose to do what pleases our old nature instead, we have that extra push from the holy spirit working in us that guides our footsteps toward the will of God.

There's also the aspect of the free will choice to be self-controlled. This comes across in numerous ways, including:

- Being choosy about the company we keep.
- Being disciplined about what we seek for entertainment.
- Avoiding things that trigger our impulse to sin.
- Filling our heads with godly principles rather than worldly missives.
- Making the decision to concern ourselves with God's opinion over the world's.
- Practicing self-denial and getting comfortable with not having the things we want, the way we want them, especially if our desires are contradictory to God's commandments.

Self-control, like anything, becomes a habit the more we choose to do it. The more we choose to say "yes" to the things of God and "no" to shoveling stuff into the bottomless hole of our sin nature, the easier it is to keep saying "yes." Over time, we train ourselves to be self-controlled in every aspect of our lives.

This is the ultimate sacrifice we can give in return to the one who sacrificed his life for us; it's how we *live* as sacrifices, holy before God: by denying and dying to ourselves and our own wants so we can live for Him. That may seem overwhelming, but just remember: it starts with saying yes to the things of God just once.

And then once more.

And then once more.

TAKE ACTION:

Take a good, hard look at an aspect of your life, spiritual or otherwise, where you lack self-control. What is one thing you can do *today* to bring that area of your life into submission and better yourself through it?

MARRIAGE

MARRIAGE, I HAVE FOUND, IS one of the most changing and challenging things in life.

Each year I'm married to my childhood sweetheart, my best friend, I learn new aspects of why marriage is so important. It's not just about me, not just about my feelings, not just about my happiness. It's not just him, his feelings, or his happiness, either.

Marriage makes us better people *and* better servants of Jesus, because in the course of it we are learning more and more about how our union is meant to reflect deeper spiritual realities. But it's a daily fight against the selfishness of the carnal nature, in order to live an Ephesians 5 kind of love—the kind where we are each putting the other's needs first so both are taken care of and we are serving and honoring God in the model of Christ and his bride, the Church.

It's true, what everyone says: marriage is hard, it's work, and it's a lifelong commitment to something bigger than yourself. But the beauty is that God wants marriage to succeed. So you can trust He is in it with you and your spouse—a solid foundation that, when built upon properly, will outlast any of the storms and seasons and challenges of life.

What is Marriage?

Merriam-Webster Dictionary defines **marriage** as "the state of being united as spouses in a consensual and contractual relationship recognized by law."

However, in the eyes of God, marriage is much more than that. It is a threefold cord of husband, wife, and God, and a union of body, heart, and soul between the two parties that should not be severed except under the gravest circumstances—such as when one spouse breaks their vows and becomes abusive.

Marriage is a covenant that reflects spiritual realities and therefore should not be undertaken lightly, but with the utmost sincerity and commitment; because when a Christian couple enters into that union, they are in essence committing to the responsibility of acting as a reflection of how Christ behaves with the Church and vice versa.

Marriage is enormously important to God—so much so that He used it as an allegory for His relationship with His chosen people, Israel, and now again to explain the way of Christ with the Church.

What Does the Bible Say About Marriage?

Genesis 2:24: "Therefore a man shall leave his father and his mother and hold fast to his wife, and they shall become one flesh."

Proverbs 18:22 - He who finds a wife finds what is good and receives favor from the LORD.

Colossians 3:18-19 - Wives, submit yourselves to your husbands, as is fitting in the Lord. Husbands, love your wives and do not be harsh with them.

How Can I Build a Stronger Marriage?

There are many wonderful tools that help marriages grow stronger, varying from couples' devotionals and marital exercises to marriage conferences, retreats, and even counseling. Whatever stage your marriage is in—even if you are engaged but not yet married!—it's important not to just assume the marriage will "take care of itself" as long as no glaring issues arise.

More than perhaps any other relationship, marriage requires maintenance and attention from both parties. It requires active love, emotional and physical intimacy, and a partnership essence between two people with God at the center in order to be truly, deeply, lastingly healthy. Making the marriage a priority, particularly when jobs, children, hobbies, etc. are in the picture, is also essential to keeping the relationship stable and prosperous.

One of the best ways to ensure a healthy marriage is to measure yours and your spouse's behavior against the standard of Ephesians 5, which lays out the important roles that both husband and wife play in the relationship. This passage beautifully describes not only the unique temporal aspects of the marriage, but also the crucial spiritual realities paralleled and involved.

In short, what God asks of husband and wife in Ephesians 5 is to lay aside the priority of self and care first and foremost for one another.

When both parties live in this sacrificial mindset, it reflects the spiritual reality—Christ dying for us, thus we die to ourselves and live for him—and it ensures that both parties are taken care of, because both are prioritizing the needs of the other over their own.

TAKE ACTION:

If you're married, what can you do *this week* to make your marriage a priority through the chaos of life?

If you're unmarried, take a moment to read passages about Jesus and the Church, such as Ephesians 5. What can you glean about the devoted life of Jesus to his Body from these passages, and what can you do to live more fully for him this week?

FAMILY

THE DESIRE FOR FAMILY IS a need rooted deep in every human heart. It's something we gravitate toward almost unconsciously from a very young age. I believe it's so important to us because it is so important to the One in whose image we're created!

Think about this: our very reason for existing—as a species, as a Body of Christ—is because God desired a family so much that He created us; and then He gave His only Son in sacrifice to redeem us from death.

Reflecting that deeper spirituality, human beings long for the depth of relationship that comes from family...which is why if we don't find it in our birth family, we often seek it in different ways. Tight spiritual circles, interest groups, gangs, sports teams, tribes, cliques—they all have something in common: they replicate the acceptance and belonging of family. Some do it in healthy ways, others far from it, but roughly speaking all exist to meet the same basic need: we want to be loved, we want to belong.

What a blessing to know that regardless of the status of our earthly family, we have a heavenly one waiting to welcome us with open arms. With God as the Father and fellow Christians as our brothers and sisters, we have the promise of an eternal family that shares the same love, the same spirit, the same brother Jesus and the same glorious future.

If you too are a follower of Jesus, I am so happy to call you family. And I am so thrilled that one day we will all be dining at the same table of our glorious Father and our wonderful Brother, and that we will be one.

WHAT IS FAMILY?

Merriam-Webster Dictionary defines **family** as "the basic unit in society traditionally consisting of two parents rearing their children; also any of various social units differing from but regarded as equivalent to the traditional family."

The family unit is very important to God. Like marriage, familyhood parallels important spiritual realities. The Body of Christ is a family, and the healthy family unit should reflect the way of God and Jesus with the Church. In the time of the biblical accounts, society was structured around the family, which was usually a closely-knit and multigenerational conglomerate where everyone looked after everyone else.

In our society, where independence and making one's own way are highly valued and it's not at all uncommon for families to live across the country or even on separate continents from one another, there's often a loss of close familial ties.

It's important that we strive even harder to maintain those bonds so we don't miss out on the powerful spiritual and moral lessons and blessings that can be gleaned from the strong and committed family structure.

WHAT DOES THE BIBLE SAY ABOUT FAMILY?

Ephesians 6:1 - Children, obey your parents in the Lord, for this is right.

Proverbs 11:29 - Whoever brings ruin on their **family** will inherit only wind, and the fool will be servant to the wise.

Ephesians 6:4 - Fathers, do not exasperate your children; instead, bring them up in the training and instruction of the Lord.

HOW CAN I STRENGTHEN MY FAMILY TIES?

Family love in the Greco-Roman world was often referred to by the word *storgē*. This is the kind of love Christians are urged to have for one another, but in order to make family a priority, we have to apply a great deal of *agape* love as well, putting the family's needs before our own.

For this reason, family-orientation in our attitude requires a conscious reaching out and effort to foster relationships, heal hurts, and maintain contact, particularly if distance separates us.

We should also be mindful to keep God in the forefront. Christian parents model the Jesus-following life to their children not just by sending them to Sunday School, but by inviting God into the midst of family matters with prayer, praise, etc., and by demonstrating the importance of God-fearing life by their own actions.

After all, God's love is the glue that binds the family together.

Children are told to: Respect, honor, and heed their parents, learning from their wisdom. Never to curse or strike them.

Parents are told to: Train up, care for, and instruct their children. Never to taunt or provoke them for a reaction.

Some other things we need to be focused on in order to strengthen family ties are:

- **Love.** The family must be rooted and grounded in the love of God and Jesus. Love is the greatest witness, the most important teacher, and the thing that everyone craves most from an early age. The lack of love is so harmful it can distort a child's formative years and negatively impact the entire rest of their life. Conversely, a family built on an outpouring of godly love will be supernaturally strengthened from the inside out and be much better able to support one another and be a greater blessing to those they come into contact with.

- **Forgiveness.** The closer we are to people, the more we open ourselves up to be hurt by them. There isn't a family on earth that hasn't had some kind of hurt, misunderstanding, or other offense in their midst. Willingness to reconcile and forgive is an imperative part to ensuring the wholeness of the family unit.

- **Humility.** This goes for parents, children, and all other members of the family unit. Just as children are encouraged to confess to their mistakes and own up to them, parents should not be afraid to admit to their children when they make a mistake and ask for their forgiveness, too. This kind of sincere two-way communication from both parents and children fosters a deeper trust and understanding of one another.

- **Honesty.** Building a trustworthy foundation of honesty within the family is critical to its success and endurance in the long run. This requires each person to bring forward their struggles, the others to love and to listen empathically, and then the family to tackle problems as a team.

- **Patience.** Every person in the family unit will have their own unique struggles and trials to endure. Having patience with others when they're facing these challenges and encouraging and supporting rather than becoming aggravated helps keep the family unit tight and hearts tender toward one another.

Family ties are complex and often in a state of flux. As children grow and mature, issues flush to the surface and must be dealt with. Parents aging, siblings taking different life roads, new children, grandchildren, nieces, nephews, cousins, etc. coming into the mix, all influence the dynamic. But when we make love and godliness the compass by which we chart our course together, the family unit has a much better chance of thriving.

WORDS OF LIFE

TAKE ACTION:

What steps can you take to prioritize your family life this week?

WORK

IT'S HARD TO TURN ONE way or another without catching an earful of someone telling you how to relate to the concept of work. Everything from "Get a job you love doing every day" to "do whatever work you have to so you can retire early and enjoy the rest of your life."

But work is so much bigger than the job we do to earn money. While we are doing our "day job", we also have a job to do for God—one from which we will never retire, that has no end no matter our age, health, or any other circumstance.

What's important about our work is that whatever we're doing, we do it in such a way that we honor God, and either simultaneously or additionally make time to fulfill the commission—the eternal work—He's given us.

So we should often be assessing: am I paying enough attention to the work of the Lord? Am I approaching all the work of my life with balanced focus and attention to the things that matter?

I'm here to serve God. How's that "working" out?

WHAT IS WORK?

Merriam-Webster Dictionary defines **work** (in this context) as "activity in which one exerts strength or faculties to do or perform something; activity that a person engages in regularly to earn a livelihood."

The Bible addresses the subject of work in various ways and in many different contexts, including: the work we do for God, the work we do for a living, and the kind of work we will do for eternity. The culture of biblical times was extremely labor-intensive, as there was no such concept as retirement for the common person; they worked until they were not physically able, and then their family's livelihood was often taken up by the children and continued on into the next generation.

God is very clear about the kind of work He expects His people to do and about the attitude we should present in a working environment. This subject is extremely crucial in this day and age, when often people are trapped in jobs they dislike and wondering how to behave in a godly manner in such environments and in their relationships there.

It's important to remember that regardless of where we work or how we feel about our job, we are still representing Christ—and we need to show up in a way that serves as a good witness for him.

WHAT DOES THE BIBLE SAY ABOUT WORK?

1 Corinthians 15:58 - Therefore, my dear brothers and sisters, stand firm. Let nothing move you. Always give yourselves fully to the **work** of the Lord, because you know that your **labor** in the Lord is not in vain.

Ephesians 6:5-9 – Servants, be obedient to those who are your masters according to the flesh with fear and trembling, *and* with a sincere heart, as *you are* to Christ. *Be obedient* not only to win their approval when they are watching you, but as servants of Christ, doing the will of God from the *depths of your* soul, serving with a good attitude, as to the Lord and not to people, knowing that whatever good anyone does, he will be paid back the same from the Lord, whether *he is* a slave or *is* free. And masters, act the same *way* toward them. Stop threatening *them*, because you know that he who is both their Lord and yours is in heaven, and there is no partiality with him.

2 Thessalonians 3:10 - For even when we were with you, we gave you this rule: "The one who is unwilling to **work** shall not eat."

How Can I Become A Better Worker?

God makes it clear, particularly in places like Colossians and Ephesians, that in whatever work we do, we should do it as if we were personally serving Him. This doesn't mean we should stay in abusive or dishonest work environments, but simply that when we do labor, we should remember it's not about earning praise from—or pleasing the whims of—other people; we should be glorifying *God* with our work ethic.

In the Book of Proverbs, God rebukes the mindset of a sluggard, one who does the bare minimum just to get by. In order to do work in a way that's pleasing to God and brings honor and glory to Him, we must be willing to give our best effort and conduct ourselves in ways above reproach, regardless of how our coworkers are behaving.

Many people struggle with the feeling that if they are not doing "Christian work"—such as pastoring a church, working for a Christian ministry, or leading a worship team—then they aren't really *working for God*. But God makes it clear that while He calls some to service in ministry, He also needs His people in other positions bringing His truth to all different social spheres.

We see this represented biblically as well. Before his ministry began, Jesus was likely working his family business, serving both the faithful and faithless; yet we can be certain his attitude had a lasting impact on both kinds of people.

The apostles held various positions of labor, including fishing, before and briefly after following Jesus's ministry.

We see throughout Scripture how people like Ruth, David, and Joseph were going about their business of gathering wheat, tending flocks, and serving in wealthy houses and prison yards...yet their work gained them favor and mention in the chronicles of time.

None of these were considered glamorous jobs at the time. They were simply part of day-to-day living; these were not rabbis and high priests, yet they were working their hearts out—and in many cases, serving God in the field of their labor.

We too can do the work of the Lord even if we are not exclusively serving His people, because working for God is a matter of attitude, not job title or position.

- For those in positions of service, God makes it clear they're to serve with humility and sincere hearts, as if they were serving Him.
- For those in positions of leadership, God warns that they should treat those subordinate to them with humility and sincere hearts as well, because God is impartial to both positions.

Whether we work as bosses or employees, we should always represent God in just, honest, humble, and kind ways, so that He receives glory through our conduct.

TAKE ACTION:

How can you better serve and represent God in your job this week?

RELATIONSHIP (WITH GOD)

ONE OF THE THINGS I find saddest in the world is just how few people understand they can have a real *relationship* with God.

Within so many denominations and factions of Christianity, God is presented as a distant, often angry figure who we serve out of deep respect and often fear, but rarely with warmth or mutual affection. Verses about God's sacrificial and tender fatherly love are overshadowed by teachings of hellfire, brimstone, and an angry God based largely on Old Testament passages.

Worse than the fact that many Christians think they can't have a relationship with God is that they don't *want* one. Not with a God like that.

Yet at its core, relationship with God—and with others—is the reason for our very existence. It is through relationship with Him that we discover a sense of purpose and peace beyond what our day-to-day life imparts. When we lack this relationship, it resonates in us like smacking a bone on wood—it vibrates through us and everything else goes strangely numb. Christian artist Plumb described this sense as "a God-shaped hole"...and the restless soul is indeed searching for Him.

Do you have a true, personal, intimate relationship with God?

Do you fear it? Desire it?

Because I guarantee you, He desires to have one with *you*.

WHAT IS OUR RELATIONSHIP WITH GOD?

Our relationship with God is established scripturally as primarily that of Father/child and Master/servant. While those two concepts may seem dichotomous to our modern way of thinking, in the culture of the time when the biblical accounts took place, they actually weren't quite so different from one another.

In ancient cultures, the father was the head of the household, which made him the voice of the family, the decision-maker, and the one to whom everyone under the roof answered. Like in Greco-Roman culture, if the father said the sky was purple, everyone in the family would agree and operate under this conclusion as fact and law!

In a similar way, servants were subject to their Lord or Master's leading. Where he told them to go, they went, and what he told them to do, they did. So, when the Bible defines our relationship with God by these parameters, there is actually no division in mindset.

As both children and servants of God, we are called to follow His leading unquestioningly. In return, we are treated as beloved sons and daughters, indispensable members of His family adopted into His purposes by His abounding grace and love.

What Does the Bible Say About Our Relationship with God?

John 3:16 - For God so loved the world that He gave His only begotten Son, that whoever believes in Him should not perish but have everlasting life.

1 Peter 5:7 - Cast all your anxiety on him because he cares for you.

Romans 8:31-32 - What, then, shall we say in response to these things? If God is for us, who can be against us? He who did not spare his own Son, but gave him up for us all — how will he not also, along with him, graciously give us all things?

How Can I Become Closer to God?

The first step toward becoming closer to God is to make your relationship with Him a priority. Just like any relationship, if we let it stagnate and don't give proper care and attention to nourishing and nurturing it, we will eventually drift apart. So, if we don't prioritize our relationship with God, eventually we'll begin to feel distance between us.

While God seeks a deeper relationship with us, He will not "force" us to spend time with Him. He may press upon our hearts, but as the saying goes, "God is a gentleman." He will not compel our relationship with Him; otherwise, it wouldn't truly be a relationship with real interaction. We must be willing to meet Him halfway, like in any relationship.

Some of the ways we can become closer to God are by: reading His Word; spending time in prayer and meditating on the things He deems important; spending time both praising and worshiping Him. training ourselves to speak of Him honestly and openly; calling Him by His name, Yahweh!

TAKE ACTION:

How can you make your relationship with God a priority this week?

RELATIONSHIP (WITH JESUS)

IN HIS WONDERFUL BOOK "Considering Jesus", Dan Gallagher refers to a survey he took of random people he crossed paths with. Among many he interviewed about their outlook on Christianity, countless folks had problems with Christians and even with God, yet with Jesus they were just fine.

This concept both surprises me and makes perfect sense. In a way, it flawlessly reflects the spiritual reality we learn about in 1 Timothy 2:5 – Jesus is the mediator between man and God. Not just in how he died for us, but between opinionated humanity and the God we often struggle to comprehend.

Jesus, a man like us, tempted in all the same ways, struggling with the same pain and doubt and fear and all the emotions we comprehend, makes *sense* to us.

This is why a relationship with Jesus is so important. Without that model of his life, that fathoming of right living and love, that bridge between us and the Father, life is so much more terrifying, more empty, more difficult.

Relationship with Jesus makes sense of the infinite. He is our mediator, our bridge, our brother.

And relationship with him is vital to our spiritual, mental, and emotional wellbeing.

What is Our Relationship with Jesus?

Our relationship with Jesus is established scripturally as primarily that of siblings and Lord/servant. It can seem confusing at first that our relationships with both God and Jesus have a Lord/servant aspect, but Ephesians 1 establishes this well when saying that after Jesus' resurrection, God placed everything under his feet. Now we, the Church, follow Christ as well as God, because they are one in purpose.

As the Son of God, Jesus is also our brother, because we are the *adopted* sons and daughters of God. This familial bond is further demonstrated in that we are co-heirs in the Kingdom of God.

But Jesus is also called a Shepherd, the Head of the Body of Christ (of which we are all a part), our Savior, and the Way through which we come to God. He is the cornerstone of our redemption story—the key to our eternal survival.

What Does the Bible Say About Our Relationship with Jesus?

John 14:6 - "I am the way, and the truth, and the life. No one comes to the Father except through me."

Hebrews 4:15 - For we do not have a high priest who is unable to empathize with our weaknesses, but one who has been tempted in every way just as *we are, yet* without sin.

Romans 5:6 - For while we were still weak, at the right time Christ died in place of the ungodly.

How Can I Become Closer with Jesus?

Just like our relationship with God, our relationship with Jesus is one we must prioritize and tend to in order for it to strengthen and grow.

We must make specific time for him, a place in our sanctuary where he is our focus without the distractions of life. We also approach Jesus in many similar ways as we do God, such as:

- Reading the words of Jesus in the Four Gospels and reading about him in other places, like Psalm 101, Isaiah 42:1-4; Isaiah 49:1-6; Isaiah 50:4-7; Isaiah 52:13-53:12; Psalm 22; and other Old Testament prophecies.
- Spending time in prayer and meditating on his teachings, like the beatitudes and parables of the Gospels.
- Spending time both praising and worshiping him.
- Practicing the manifestations of the holy spirit, which is the "helper" Jesus promised to his followers in the Gospel of John.
- Training ourselves to speak of Jesus as our savior, our brother and leader, the greatest

hero in history and our wonderful teacher and friend.

We also strengthen our relationship with Jesus by following the instructions he has laid out for us and by honoring the great commission he gave to his Church: to go out into the world and make disciples in his name.

When we are doing the work of Jesus by walking in the revelation of God, we strengthen that unique bond with him. Jesus laid this principle out clearly for his followers in the Gospel of John when he said, "You are my friends if you do the things that I command you. No longer do I call you servants, for the servant does not know what his lord is doing. But I have called you friends because all that I have heard from my Father I have made known to you."

TAKE ACTION:

What can you do to strengthen your relationship with Jesus this week?

RELATIONSHIP (WITH THE BODY OF CHRIST)

THE IMPORTANCE OF FAMILY EXTENDS further than just our blood relations or our close friends.

Human beings are built for relationship. The way we interact with God, Jesus, the people around us, and even ourselves has a defining effect on our lives. If we are out of balance in any relationship in our lives, it tends to have a ripple effect on other areas as well. We should always be in a proactive assessment of our relationships to ensure that we are in a healthy, balanced, active state. When we prioritize relationships and their importance, it better equips us to fulfill our calling in the Body of Christ.

Family is a concept we were created for, and it's actualized in practice in the Body of Christ.

Not all Christians always feel that close connection within the Body. Like any family, there have been schisms, division, disagreements—the awkwardest of awkward "holiday dinners" with enough hate and insults flung to scare off any newcomer and even convince some of the siblings to remove themselves from future get-togethers.

But when it's walked out in the healthy way portrayed for us through the epistles, like in Ephesians where we're told about the "unity of the spirit in the bond of peace", the Body of Christ provides safety, shelter, support, love, community, connection, and a sense of purpose—the core of relationship and family.

Maybe you've been holding the Body of Christ at arm's length, burned by one too many arguments at the family table. Maybe you've felt you can do it better, just you and God, on your own...that you don't need relationship or family.

But we are called into more than just a commission from God; we are called to be in relationship with each other, conducting ourselves in the manner of Christ, walking in love and building one another up, urging each other to greater and greater works and a deeper understanding of *our* purpose within *God's* purpose.

If you've walked away, I invite you to pray for and seek a holistic, healthy Christian community to invest your heart in. With all my heart, I ask you to return, to be with your brothers and sisters, to seek the unity of the spirit in the bond of peace.

I invite you to come home.

What is Our Relationship with The Body of Christ?

The Body of Christ is our family. Christians of every denomination are our brothers and sisters. We were each adopted into this family when we accepted Christ as our Lord.

In Galatians 6:10, Christians are instructed to be "especially good to the household of faith," and to do things particularly *for* "one another"—like bear one another's burdens, be subject to one another, be devoted to one another, speak truth to one another, and love one another. We are also tasked with maintaining the unity of the spirit in the bond of peace.

We are fellow-laborers and fellow-ambassadors spreading the Gospel message and reaping the harvest of that work, and we strive in tandem with one another under Christ, who is the Head directing members of his Body. Each of us is called to a different role, or "function," within the Body, and we're called to encourage, uplift, and help one another fulfill those roles.

What Does the Bible Say About Our Relationship with The Body of Christ?

Ephesians 4:2-3 - Be completely humble and gentle; be patient, bearing with one another in love. Make every effort to keep the unity of the spirit through the bond of peace.

Hebrews 10:24-25 - And let us consider one another, to spur one another on to love and good works, not abandoning our meeting together, as some are in the habit of doing, but exhorting one another, and all the more as you see the Day drawing near.

Ephesians 9:19-21 - So then you are no longer strangers and foreigners, but you are fellow-citizens with the holy ones and members of the household of God, having been built on the foundation of the apostles and prophets, Christ Jesus himself being the cornerstone, in whom the whole building, being fitted together, grows into a holy sanctuary in the Lord, in whom you also are being built together by means of the spirit into a dwelling place of God.

How Can I Become Closer to the Body of Christ?

While the reality of our place in the Body of Christ is constant, we may still feel adrift or alone at times, particularly if we have no church or fellowship to attend. While having those opportunities certainly helps us feel closer to the Body, it's more our actions when we're present with one another that foster a sense of community.

A few ways we can become closer with our fellow Christians in any setting are:

Speak Well of One Another: As members of Christ's Body, we do a disservice to the whole Body when we speak poorly about each other. We are all told that, having learned Christ, we should not let defaming speech come from our mouths.

This is in regard to everyone, but particularly to fellow Christians. We may have arguments with certain denominations or the practices within them, but the loving and Christlike thing to do is not to go around slandering them to anyone who'll listen! It's to confront the problem where it arises. When we tell everyone but the person we have an issue with *about* that issue, we tear down the Body of Christ rather than healing it or bringing about necessary change.

Speak the Truth In Love: When we do confront our fellow Christians, it needs to be from a place of love. Our words must be full of grace, pure, and intended to encourage change or reformation as needed, not to just to air our grievances and get them off our chest.

When we speak to our brothers and sisters in Christ with the truths we know, but without the love of Jesus, then Jesus *himself* tells us we are ineffective. We strengthen the bonds within the Body when we speak in love.

Seek Unity: We will never have unity in the sense that we will find other Christians with whom we share 100% of the same values and beliefs, which might somehow make life perfect. What we have and what we are told to maintain is not unity in doctrine, but unity *in the spirit.* That means recognizing we are all saved by the same Jesus, who is our peace, and we all have the same holy spirit, which is our common ground. That's what unifies us.

Rather than arguing with our fellow Jesus-followers, we should be doing everything in our power to maintain unity. Jesus tells us people will know we follow him by the love we have for one another; we need to live and walk out the unity of the spirit in a way that makes the Gospel message and the family of God attractive, not repulsive, to others.

Live With *Agape* Love: This is the kind of selfless and other-centered love God holds toward us. *Agape* love equips us to do what is necessary for the wellbeing of others.

While we are also told to have brotherly and familial love toward the Body of Christ, these are "feeling" loves; at the same time, we should be loving toward those in the Body of Christ with whom we do not "feel" kinship. That is the *agape*, the "doing" love.

TAKE ACTION:

What is a "one another" action you can do for a brother or sister in Christ this week? Go out and boldly accomplish it!

COURAGE

ONE OF MY MOST TREASURED possessions is a signed copy of a beloved novel, *The Traitor Prince*. Inside the front cover, hand-scrawled by the author herself, is the phrase that sealed this story forever in my heart and soul: *Fear out. Courage in.*

Courage has been a theme in my life since a family trip to Colorado in 2017 when it became clear to me how fear above all else had become my guide through life. And I was *done* with all that nonsense. Slowly but surely ever since, I have been unspooling the reel of courage wrapped tight within myself—stuffed away through pain and heartache and the subsequent unleashing of an anxiety disorder that progressed through my adolescence until I received deliverance in 2020.

Seizing hold of courage has allowed me to write the books of my heart, travel solo, teach in front of a crowd, begin a small business, seek therapy, become a mother, and step boldly into my calling from the Creator Himself.

Courage is not optional if we are going to walk the path God has called us to, because persecution is not optional, either. To withstand the latter, we must have the former. But human bravery often falters in the face of spiritual onslaught; even Jesus wept at what was to come for him in the torture and hanging on the cross.

We find our courage exactly where he found his—in the hope and promises and strength of God. Ultimately, we must choose what we will focus on: the fear of tomorrow or the God who holds it.

Choose God. Choose bravery. Choose the next step.

Exhale earthly fear. Inhale heavenly courage.

WHAT IS COURAGE?

Merriam-Webster Dictionary defines **courage** as "mental or moral strength to venture, persevere, and withstand danger, fear, or difficulty." A more widely-used definition is that courage is "the presence of fear, yet the willingness to carry on."

Each of us will endure things in this life that require courage; it can be anything from a battlefield to a threatening situation to a necessary conversation/confrontation, or a struggle with mental or physical illness, grief, etc. Courage is not demanded only of those facing physical harm, but also of anyone who stands to incur injury, hurt, or struggle from the path they choose or the things inflicted on them.

Jesus warned his followers that they'd face difficult times, persecution, scorn, and worse. It takes courage to face those things and not become jaded, hopeless, or led astray...so no wonder the Bible admonishes us over and over to have courage!

WHAT DOES THE BIBLE SAY ABOUT COURAGE?

Deuteronomy 31:6: Be strong and of **good courage**, do not fear nor be afraid of them; for the LORD your God, He is the One who goes with you. He will not leave you nor forsake you.

John 16:33: I have told you these things so that, in union with me, you have peace. In the world you will have hardships, but **have courage**; I have overcome the world.

1 Corinthians 16:13: Be watchful, stand fast in the faith, **be courageous**, be strong...

How Can I Become More Courageous?

While anyone can fake bravery in times of crisis, true courage comes from having our feet planted in Truth. Understanding the power of our God, the importance of the spiritual battle, and the promises of the future enables us to not just plaster on a smile in difficult times, but to draw strength to stand and stay in the fight.

- When we firmly grasp the magnitude of the love and promises of God, it broadens our perspective.

- When we submit ourselves to Him, we put aside the need for false, showy bravery and accept Him as our strength.
- When we lean on Him to guide our steps, and hide His Word in our hearts, we can step boldly into difficult confrontations.
- When we trust the future that is ensured through our salvation, the trials of this life consume less of us.
- When we truly comprehend the magnitude of the love He has lavished on us and how precious we are in His sight, the opinions of others grow dim.
- And when we fathom the enormity of His commission to us, the vastness of His grace, and that the very souls of people are at stake just as ours once were, it becomes more crucial and more personal than ever that we live with Christlike love and courage, no matter the cost.

Ultimately, it is by knowing God through and through, from past to present to future hope, that we learn to have courage that surpasses any challenge we face in this life.

TAKE ACTION:

What is one area of your life where you need more courage? Which of God's promises will help you grow your courage and conquer this area?

WISDOM

THE START OF 2020 BROUGHT a lot of reflection. It was the end of one decade and the start of a whole new one. All across social media, posts cropped up comparing 2010 to 2020, showing the "glow up" as people aged from their awkward teen years into adulthood.

In my own reflection, one thing become utterly clear: the biggest difference between 2010 Renee and 2020 Renee is she realized she's not as wise as she thought when she was 16-17.

Somehow teenagers always seem to think they have it figured out, and I was no different; I thought I was really wise and savvy back then, especially compared to my peers. 26-year-old me laughed at that naivety, while bearing in mind that 36-year-old me is going to have a laugh of her own when she rereads this someday (if she can bring herself to!).

But here's the thing; 16-year-old me was certainly wiser than 6-year-old me. And 26-year-old me came quite a ways further. And 36, 46, and 56-year-old me will all have their own fresh perspective to share on wisdom.

Because wisdom is not something we attain at some point in life and find ourselves with a full cup, nothing more to learn and nowhere else to grow. We grow in wisdom as we make wise choices and pursue knowledge, activities, and investments that increase our prudence.

The Hebrew word for "wisdom" occurs nearly 40 times within the 31 chapters of the Book of Proverbs alone...a fairly clear indication that this is not a concept God takes lightly. Over and over, He admonishes people to make good, wise choices; to not just sit around on their hands waiting to become wise, but to get up and actively *pursue* wisdom, like they'd search for buried treasure and valuable jewels.

Why this reiteration, and why so much effort and emphasis on the subject? Because not only does wisdom enable us to walk rightly before our God, but it's with wisdom that we are able to live the best version of our lives. Wisdom keeps us out of a lot of bad situations, prolongs our lives, enables us to counsel others, and helps steer the course of not only our circumstances, but even the world we effect—all in a better, more godly direction.

Living with a lack of wisdom is like leaving a door open for suffering; sooner or later, our "lucky" poor choices will run out, and all we're left with is misery.

Instead of living life on the edge, hoping for the best, make time and effort to *pursue* wisdom; seek it in the pages of Scripture and from those who are themselves wise and learned.

Never stop seeking it, no matter how much you have or how much you know. Seek it above all else. You will never be disappointed!

WHAT IS WISDOM?

Merriam-Webster Dictionary defines **wisdom** as "ability to discern inner qualities and relationships; good sense, judgement."

Wisdom is vital to every person at every stage of life. It is also something we can choose to seek and heed, or forsake at our own risk.

Wisdom is imperative to our safety from a young age; it also factors heavily into how we approach life choices such as relationships, careers, monetary or asset investments, and more.

The more we exercise wisdom, the more likely we are to have positive outcomes. But wisdom isn't something that simply appears to us one day; it is gained through life experiences and by actively seeking it—in Scripture, in relationship with God, and from others.

What Does the Bible Say About Wisdom?

James 1:5 - But if any of you lacks **wisdom**, let him ask God *for it*, who gives to everyone generously and without finding fault, and it will be given to him.

Proverbs 8:35 - Because the one finding [**wisdom**] finds life, and he will obtain favor from Yahweh.

Proverbs 4:5-7 - Get **Wisdom**! Get understanding! [...] **Wisdom** is the principal thing, *so* get **Wisdom**; and with all your purchases, purchase understanding.

How Can I Become Wiser?

Scripture itself is a tremendous, unmatched source of wisdom. There is much we can learn about the principles of life and how to navigate this world by reading the Bible, particularly Proverbs and the Gospels.

But really, the entire Bible is for our learning, both the Old and New Testaments; and through the experiences of our forefathers we can glean many insights into what behavior is profitable and what is detrimental or outright dangerous.

Another way which we attain wisdom is directly from God. This happens through one of the manifestations of the gift of holy spirit, often called a "word" or "message" of Wisdom (1 Cor. 12:8). A message of wisdom involves God or Jesus providing direction or guidance on how to apply our present knowledge about a matter. This message differs from our personal "knowledge bank" in that it comes at God's discretion.

We must be careful not to mistake all kinds of wisdom mentioned in the Bible as a "message of wisdom" that will appear whenever we need to act wisely. God instructs us throughout the Bible, and particularly in the Book of Proverbs, to actively pursue wisdom throughout our lives and learn to apply it ourselves!

A third way to gain wisdom is through learning from the right people. One of the beauties of mentorship is that we can learn from someone who's walked the road before us; through their learning, their attempts, triumphs, and failures, we may save ourselves a lot of heartache and foolishness along the way.

If there's an area where you lack wisdom, don't be afraid to seek out a mentor who can impart their wisdom to you!

TAKE ACTION:

What is an area of your life where you could exercise more wisdom? What is one step you can take this week toward exercising godly principles in that area?

FAITH/TRUST

TRUST. FAITH. SUCH VITAL ASPECTS of our spiritual walk, and yet for many Christians they're overlooked. It's entirely possible to serve God out of fealty, devotion, or fear—but still not necessarily trust Him. And in those relationships, there is a deeper sense of something missing.

The reason trust in God is so important is because if we do not really trust Him to lead us, guide us, and speak to us, to care for our needs and be our provision and sufficiency, then we can't have an actual grounded relationship with Him.

I used to think having love and devotion was enough to keep any relationship—like a marriage, for example—sailing steady. But it's not. I've loved my husband every day since we started dating, but it was only when I really began to *trust* him that I started to feel secure and open in our relationship; that I began to show him the sides of me that weren't just happy, bubbly, and nice. Because I trusted him, I let down my walls and let the harder, harsher, and hurt pieces show through—and he was able to help me start healing those things.

So it is with God. All the warm, fuzzy feelings in the world amount to nothing if we don't have a solid foundation of trust to shore it up. In order for God to work in us, with us, to heal us and help us grow, we must trust Him deeply enough to open up our hearts and lives. Even the ugly parts.

It's written deep within the human heart to desire wholeness and relationship, to be understood and loved. And to reach that depth in relationship with God, we must build up an unshakeable trust in Him.

Luckily, He makes it so easy to do with the countless ways He shows himself faith*ful*.

WHAT IS FAITH/TRUST?

There is actually an important distinction between these two things!

The word "faith" in the Bible often refers to how we relate to God Himself. We are told to have faith in Him, in His promises, etc. "Faith" in these contexts is translated from the Latin *fides* which replaced the Greek *pistis*—actually more accurately translated "trust"—when the Bible was translated into the Latin language. So, in many places where we are told to "have faith" in something, God is actually asking us to have *trust*. That's an important difference!

Merriam-Webster Dictionary defines **"faith"** as "firm belief in something for which there is no proof," whereas it labels **"trust"** as "assured reliance on the character, ability, strength, or truth of someone or something." So it must be understood that God isn't asking us to believe in things for which there isn't proof; He's asking us to *trust Him* based on His reliable character.

What Does the Bible Say About Faith/Trust?

Romans 3:28 - For we maintain it is by **trust** that a person is declared righteous, apart from works of law.

Ephesians 2:8 - For by grace you have been saved through **trust**, and this is not from yourselves, it is the gift of God.

Galatians 3:26 - For you are all sons of God through **trust** in Christ Jesus.

How Can I Become More Trusting?

This is the crux of why the distinction between faith/trust is so important. If we rely on the common definition of faith, the only way to have "more faith" is to throw yourself more completely onto the unproven belief that there is something out there that will catch you. But then our faith is utterly dependent on our ability to hope for a favorable outcome, and for most people, this only goes so far before it simply becomes impossible.

Trust, however, is something we can always grow in as we gain a deeper understanding of God's reliability, because He provides us a foundation on which to plant and grow our trust.

There is not a time in Scripture where God did not keep His word. He always works for the good of those who believe in Him. He is working out his plans and purposes for the ages, a family into which He called us. He has proved Himself loving, generous, kind, just, and wise.

How do we gain greater trust in God? By not just reading His Word, but taking necessary steps to apply and understand it; and by being in relationship with Him wherein His faithfulness proves itself not only by records from the past, but by our present reality with Him and our future together.

TAKE ACTION:

Think of a time in your life where God's actions, either through His Word or in relationship with you, increased your trust in Him. Meditate on that time. Let the memory of His reliability build up the place where your trust may have weakened since.

WORRY

WHAT'S THE BIG DEAL ABOUT WORRY?
Sometimes it's difficult to see why feeling anxious or being worried is so crippling for certain people; for Christians especially it's often all too easy to say "Just get over it. Trust God!" But worry that endures over time literally rewires the brain, creating neuropathic ruts through which the same thoughts travel again and again—and sometimes we don't

realize we're going back and forth down these tracks, wearing a system into the brain, until it's too late. Until it becomes a habit, a thought process, a pattern.

And that's exactly what the Devil wants. He knows how crippling it can truly be.

I've experienced firsthand how worry takes someone out of the game. When my anxiety was at its peak—when I was "high-octane", as my family called it, meaning I was shaking and hyperventilating and focusing all my effort on not throwing up as my brain performed the gold-metal long-jump from worst-case-scenario to *even-worse*-case scenario—I wouldn't be aware of a spiritual occurrence if it exploded in the middle of my living room. When anxiety ruled my life, I was not present, primed to hear God's voice or ready to engage His people. I was not able to fulfill my calling when I was myself filled with worry.

Even among Christians who have great trust in the Father, worry, fear, and anxiety can and do in many cases run rampant. The question is really not whether we'll face worry as we go through life—whether we'll be confronted with things, big or small, that steal our peace. That's a given. The real question is whether we will cultivate the methods for coping with these things so that we tackle them and bring them into submission—not the other way around.

WHAT IS WORRY?

Merriam-Webster Dictionary defines **worry** as "mental distress or agitation resulting from concern, usually for something impending or anticipated."

Worry, or "anxiety," ranges from concern about present or future things to mental health issues which require intervention of some kind. One medical study purports that anxiety disorders are the most common mental illness in the U.S. as of 2019, affecting 40 million adults in the United States age 18 and older, or 18.1% of the population every year.

That means that most of us probably know one or more people who deal with either generalized or aggressive anxiety. Most of these people will tell you how strange a feeling it can be. For many, it really does circulate around "what ifs", but it's not as simple as "not thinking about those things." Intrusive thoughts and fears for what tomorrow will bring can be crippling. And they can certainly make us less effective in living for Jesus.

What Does the Bible Say About Worry?

Luke 12:22 - Then Jesus said to his disciples: "Therefore I tell you, do not **worry** about your life, what you will eat; or about your body, what you will wear."

Matthew 6:27 - And which of you, by being **anxious**, is able to add one cubit to the measure of his life?

Psalm 94:19 - When **anxiety** was great within me, Your consolation brought me joy.

Philippians 4:6-7 - Do not be **anxious** about anything, but in everything by prayer and petitions, with thanksgiving, let your requests be made known to God, and then, (being in union with Christ Jesus), the peace of God, which passes all understanding, will guard your hearts and your thoughts.

How Can I Become Less Anxious?

While those with an anxiety disorder should seek treatment, whether naturopathic or pharmaceutical, so that they are not fighting an uphill battle against a chemical imbalance in the brain, there are things everyone can do to help decrease their worries and anxieties whether they have a diagnosed disorder or not.

Prioritize: Many of us struggle with worry and anxiety over what the future will bring as we see the world decline around us. But there is comfort when we prioritize our hope and promised future above the state of the world. While the things happening around us, to us, and in us can be troubling or downright *scary* at times, Jesus-followers are fighting a battle that has already been won. Whatever comes of us in this life, our future with Jesus is secure. This may not remove all the fear or trouble from today, but it certainly can help lessen our worry over what the future holds. As the saying goes, "I have no fear of what tomorrow holds, for I know Who holds tomorrow."

Dwell on the promises of God: Scripture is full of places where God and Jesus promise to be with us to the end of this age, to never leave us or forsake us, to work on our behalf, to guide, guard, and protect us. While that doesn't mean we will be free from adversity, there is comfort in knowing we do not walk through this alone.

Offer it up in prayer: We all have things we worry about, but Jesus told his disciples that worrying would not add anything to their lives. Instead, we are to bring our concerns to God in prayer, petition (asking) and in thanksgiving (for how He has taken care of us and will continue to do so). The burdens of our fear are often too big for us to carry alone, which is how we end up entrenched in worry and despair. But if we are vulnerable and humble enough to share those anxieties with God, He will lighten the burden. He is strong enough to carry it all.

Meditate on Scripture: The more of God's Word we hold in our heads and hearts, the less room there is for invasive thoughts. These pieces of Scripture also serve as spiritual swords in our hands to block the blows of worry when they start raining down on us.

Decrease screentime: With so much information at the tips of our fingers, with one click we can become aware of conflict in the remote corners of the world that our ancestors would've had no clue about.

While it's good to be informed so we can pray for things and help where we can, an oversaturation of knowledge about all the pain, loss, disease, and suffering in the world can absolutely wreck our peace. We need to be careful how much we seek these things out, especially if we're not in a position to help alleviate that suffering.

Are we devoting as much time to uplifting things as to the dark side of the world? If not, we're just asking for our anxiety to increase.

We're better off stepping back and focusing our time and energy on places we *can* help out.

TAKE ACTION:

What is something you are currently holding onto worry about? Take time to pray and give that matter up to God!

REGRET

PICTURE THE SCENE: you, snuggled up in your bed after a hard day. Your blanket is the perfect weight, your head hits the pillow juuuust right, you sink into the welcoming embrace of a comfortable mattress and—

Suddenly you remember that embarrassing thing you said at the office party six years ago or the time you waved at someone on the bus thinking they were waving at you, only they were waving at someone *behind* you, and oh great now you're wide awake with goosebumps of embarrassment coating your skin.

This is the lighter side of regret; the darker side is the pain of broken relationships, misunderstandings, falling-outs that result in real harm—physically or emotionally or spiritually—rather than just embarrassment.

Many of us will experience both in our lifetime, and they have one aspect in common: dwelling on them without action benefits absolutely nothing.

Embarrassing regret must be let go and moved on from. Guilt-based regret needs to be addressed, repented of, and also moved on from. But in order to keep regret from rearing its head again—and possibly crippling you later in life—it must be faced in a healthy, godly way.

Difficult though it may be, facing and overcoming regret is vital; without it, we can never be all that God needs us to be.

What is Regret?

Merriam-Webster Dictionary defines **regret** as "to be very sorry for." It's often used synonymously with "guilt."

Regret is something we all experience in life, because we all make mistakes. We unintentionally hurt people, do things we wish we could take back, say things we know we shouldn't have, and act out in ungodly ways that cause harm to ourselves and others. The feeling of regret at these things is often the prodding of the holy spirit, our new nature struggling with the old which always tries to find reasons to justify these behaviors.

Regret can actually be a good thing inasmuch as it compels us to rectify our wrongdoings. A healthy dose of regret prods us to repentance; the alternative is to never feel guilt when we mess up, which is evidence of a calloused heart and even a seared conscience.

But we must be careful that our guilt and regret don't turn into shame, which actually prevents us from being effective for God in the long run.

WHAT DOES THE BIBLE SAY ABOUT REGRET?

Psalm 51:9 – Hide your face from my sins, and blot out all of my guilt.

Psalm 79:8 – Do not remember against us the guilt of our ancestors. Let your tender mercies quickly meet us, for we have become very weak.

HOW DO I HANDLE REGRET IN A HEALTHY WAY?

The first step to relating to regret in a healthy way is to acknowledge the part it plays in our lives. Because no one is perfect, no one can escape wrongdoing, so we can't escape regret or guilt for those things.

The next healthy step then is to *repent* for our wrongdoing (which involves a commitment not to repeat the offense). This means taking it to God, making amends for how we sinned, and if possible, going to anyone we've wronged and apologizing and asking for forgiveness from them as well.

And then we have to *release* the regret, before it mutates into shame.

Sitting with guilt until it becomes shame is dangerous because regret says "What I did was awful," whereas shame says "*I* am awful." When we start to see our very essence as the problem, it chips away at our holistic, God-shaped view of who are in Christ and in Him.

What He wants for us is that our regret over our sin would lead to repentance and then release, so that we—and those we have hurt—can move forward without the burden of that sin hanging over our lives.

TAKE ACTION:

Is there a weight of regret or even shame you are carrying? Make the effort this week to repent and release that burden from your life!

ANGER

"MY DEFAULT IS ANGER."

I remember the surprise in myself and in my friend's expression the first time I confessed this realization to her; the first time I truly came face to face with the fact that, due to a lack of self-awareness growing up and other factors outside my control, I'd developed a default to frustration or anger at inconvenience.

For many people, anger comes naturally at the first stroke of imbalance in life. There are many things that foster this way of thinking—one of which is the notion that we shouldn't be angry at all!

This idea that especially as Christians, we should stuff our anger and put on happy faces all the time, is so harmful! What we must be conscious of with anger is to check and balance it; feeling anger at times is totally understandable, but we must control it, not allow it to control us.

We are not living in sin when we feel angry; but if anger is allowed to run amok, it can lead us to sin, and that's what we've got to watch out for.

Additionally, when anger becomes our default, we begin operating from a place of negativity, and this adversely affects our physical, mental, and even spiritual health, toxifies our environment, and ultimately it can have a seriously negative impact on our ability to live as witnesses for Christ.

The only people who want to hang out with angry people all the time are usually angry themselves; so we've got to make sure that we're keeping that anger in check and getting angry about the *right* things, not blowing up at every tiny distraction; and that when we do feel anger, we're handling it in a way that makes Jesus proud.

WHAT IS ANGER?

Merriam-Webster Dictionary defines **anger** as "a strong feeling of displeasure and usually of antagonism."

Many Christians wonder if it's wrong to be angry. In the sense of whether *feeling* anger is a sin...not in itself, no. But God warns us to get rid of all anger because danger lies in the risk that sitting in our anger will lead us to sin, due to that feeling of antagonism and displeasure. When anger drives us to hit back, that's where we're primed to step into sin.

So while we are not sinning if we *feel* angry about things, we do need to train ourselves not to fall back on anger as our first and lasting response. We don't want to invite anger and all its negative outcomes into our lives.

WHAT DOES THE BIBLE SAY ABOUT ANGER?

Ephesians 4:3 - Get rid of all bitterness and rage and **anger** and *angry* shouting and defaming speech, *along* with all malice...

Colossians 3:8 - but now you too must put away all these things: **anger**, rage, malice, defaming speech, obscene talk out of your mouth.

Ephesians 4:26 - **Be angry and** *yet* **do not sin!** Do not let the sun go down on your angry mood...

How Can I Become Less Angry?

Learning to tame anger is an arduous and truly lifelong process. While we have the power of holy spirit in us to help eradicate anger's chokehold from our lives, we will continue to struggle with it because we will always encounter things that make us feel discouraged, displeased, and a host of other emotions that can quickly morph into anger.

But just because anger will always be there does not mean we should give over to it. We have a new nature from the moment Jesus becomes our Lord, and we should always be fighting against the steep slope of anger that can lead down to sin.

One of the primary ways we do that is through redirecting our thoughts. When we find ourselves festering in anger, we have the power to lift the matter up in prayer and then shift our focus to a godly, healthy, and proactive approach.

We can also avoid anger triggers—for example, if reading or watching the news causes you to sit and stew in anger, consider cutting back or nixing your intake entirely. Or is spending time with certain individuals leaves you furious, then reconsider the company you keep.

Another key to managing anger is to recognize when we need outside help with it. Some people have a harder time dealing with their angry emotions than others, and there's no shame in seeking aid from skilled professionals or talented councilors who know techniques to keep anger from becoming a massive monster too big for us to defeat.

Ultimately, we must walk by the spirit of God. The more we are living a spirit-driven life, the less room we have for things like impatience, short-temperedness, uncontrolled and unkind behavior, etc.—all of which fuel our struggle with anger.

TAKE ACTION:

Take careful note this week of the things that make you angry. Can you avoid those triggers? For those you can't, take the matter to God and ask Him to specifically work in that area of your life to help patience and peace become your default instead.

DISCIPLINE

4 A.M. USED TO COME AWFULLY EARLY.

I wish I could say I greeted those pre-kid early morning writing sessions with grace, but more often than not when I woke up—either to a nudge from my well-trained internal clock or my alarm chirping cheerily—I sat stooped over like some soft, rumpled gargoyle ripped from her settings on the cathedral of sleep, questioning all my life choices. *All of them.*

But after thirty or so minutes of waking up in the dark, I rolled out of bed, give the oldest cat her morning treats, started the coffee and booted up my laptop. And for the next however-many-hours I hadn't wasted sitting in the bed wondering why I *do* this to myself, I wrote, and wrote, and wrote.

People often asked me how I could get up at 4 in the morning day after day, and I always told them the same thing: discipline. I loved my mornings, I loved my craft, and I loved having free time to myself in the quiet house to tell stories to the shadows around me; so I disciplined myself not to go back to sleep, not to give into that bleary-eyed haze in those long thirty minutes; and I disciplined myself to go to bed at 8 p.m. when most of my friends were just starting movies and grabbing dinner, so that I *could* get up at 4 without feeling like death warmed over.

I truly believe that in life, discipline is key; we can accomplish almost anything with the proper amount of discipline—health, strength, goals achieved, races won.

And for Christians especially, it's important we learn the art of discipline and exercise it liberally in our lives, because living with discipline in a world of excess is a vital part of pleasing God.

WHAT IS DISCIPLINE?

Merriam-Webster Dictionary defines **discipline** as "control gained by enforcing obedience or order; orderly or prescribed conduct or pattern of behavior; self-control." By its earliest definition, discipline also refers to "chastisement, training, or correction". The Bible uses both meanings.

You probably recognize one of the root words of disciplined: disciple! A well-known term among most Christians, because the disciples were people who followed the tenets of certain teachers, like Jesus. *Discipline* comes from *discipulus*, the Latin word for pupil, which also provides the source of the word *disciple*.

So for Christians, having "discipline" looks like "living as disciples of Jesus." And that does require self-discipline! Jesus called us to a higher standard of living, a better way of conduct that sets an example for the world around us. In order to live as his disciples—following his teachings and living in a way that honors him—we can't play loosely with our lives. We must stick to a code that is at times super difficult to follow...especially when our flesh nature would much rather do whatever's comfortable, fun, and/or exciting at any given moment.

WHAT DOES THE BIBLE SAY ABOUT DISCIPLINE?

Hebrews 12:11 - For the moment all **discipline** seems painful rather than pleasant, but later it yields the peaceful fruit of righteousness to those who have been trained by it.

1 Corinthians 9:27 - But I **discipline** my body and keep it under control, lest after preaching to others I myself should be disqualified.

Titus 1:8 – But [be] hospitable, a lover of good, self-controlled, upright, holy, and **disciplined**.

HOW CAN I BECOME MORE DISCIPLINED?

One of the best ways to become more disciplined in any area is to recognize that your life is not your own. Not only was every Christian's sin paid for and their life ransomed by the blood of Jesus, but when we made him our Lord, we entered into holy servitude to him. He is our Lord and Master, our Savior and King.

Historically speaking, when you were under the rule of a king, you did as the king bade you—no questions asked. So now that we serve Jesus, we are serving the King of Kings whose name is above every name. Therefore, we have no reason and no excuse not to discipline ourselves to live according to the commission, calling, and standards set forth for us.

Discipline within one's self is ultimately a choice, not a feeling, just like loving one's enemies is a choice and not a feeling. We don't do the disciplined thing because we necessarily feel like it, but because we know it's right and that's what we choose to do.

1) **Accept no excuses.** If you need to give up something in your life that's holding you back from serving God to the utmost, then take the necessary steps to do it. Don't allow excuses for certain behaviors and choices to become your Master.

2) **Hide God's words in your heart.** When the Word of the Lord is always close in our minds, convicting and correcting us, it becomes more and more difficult to make up excuses that would allow us to act in undisciplined ways.

3) **Set reminders for yourself.** Whether it's calendar notes, phone alarms, sticky notes, or whatever else works for you, be willing to go the extra mile and remind yourself to do—or not to do—certain things, until doing the RIGHT THING becomes a habit.

4) **Be accountable and willing to accept reproof.** We all have blind spots in our lives, and addressing and correcting them becomes more difficult when we refuse to heed the insight of others. Seek out trusted advice from others on the areas where you need more discipline—and accept discipline from others where necessary! This will help you become more disciplined as a whole.

Ultimately, it takes discipline (the reproof) in the areas of our lives where we struggle in order to become more disciplined (the trait) overall. The two definitions go hand in hand toward shaping us into better, more godly people and more ready disciples of our Lord Jesus Christ.

TAKE ACTION:

What is an area of your life where you lack discipline? What can you do to become more disciplined in that way specifically?

PROSPERITY

WHAT IS TRUE PROSPERITY?

For most, the notion of "prosperity" likely evokes flashes of top-line cars, mansions, and at *least* three swimming pools. When I was a kid, the Hollywood glitz and glam was certainly what prosperity looked like to me. Or at least like my friends' houses that had staircases and backyard swimming pools.

Yet as I've grown up, I've found my outlook on prosperity taking a steady shift. Do you know how many people have those material treasures and yet feel empty inside? Suicide rates are at an all-time high, and not just among the widely-labeled "destitute". Prosperity, success, to be thriving—those are actually not a standard of living. They're a way of being, flowing from the inside out.

You can have all the money and nice things in the world and not be truly prospering; and you can live a prosperous life and never set foot on a street fancier than lower-middle-class suburban.

I think of Mister Spock from Star Trek; when he bade his friends "Live long and prosper," was he really telling them to go get rich and die with pockets lined? Or was he wishing them a lengthy and fulfilling existence built on real contentment—the kind not won through money, but through peace?

Knowing Spock, probably the latter. And, come to think of it, that pointy-eared hobgoblin might've been onto something.

What is Prosperity?

Merriam-Webster Dictionary defines prosperity as "the condition of being successful or thriving."

Prosperity has become one of the most widely-discussed issues in modern Christianity—so much so that there is now a movement in many popular circles called "prosperity gospel" which teaches people to speak blessings into being by the "Word of Faith". There's a whole spate of popular preachers and televangelists who purport having the "keys" to opening the door of prosperity for their congregants, essentially by encouraging them to "positively confess" their desires into fruition.

One thing we have to be clear about is that Christian prosperity is never defined anywhere in Scripture as having everything you want in this life. In fact, we're told in many places that Christians will face persecution and troubles. It's the nature of living in a fallen world, and our belief and the gift of holy spirit in us are not guarantees of an easy life.

While a lot of people do seem to get rich and live successful lives off these "name it and claim it" practices, there's much more involved to it than first meets the eye. Occasionally the practices by which the funds or materials are acquired border on extortion or charlatanism, and God warns us that "treasures gained by wickedness profit nothing."

So we may have to shift our perspective on what it means to be "successful" or "thriving" in the first place. Is prosperity relegated to material wealth, or something more?

What Does the Bible Say About Prosperity?

Psalm 1:3 – [The one who delights in Yahweh's Law] will be like a tree planted by the streams of water that brings forth its fruit in its season, whose leaf also does not wither. And in whatever he does, he **prospers**.

2 Chronicles 32:31 - And every work that [Hezekiah] undertook in the service of the house of God and in accordance with the law and the commandments, seeking his God, he did with all his heart, and **prospered**.

Proverbs 28:25 - An arrogant soul stirs up strife, but the person who trusts in Yahweh will be made **prosperous**.

How Can I Become More Prosperous?

Scripture makes it clear that prosperity is not merely financial or material wealth we acquire by asking God for it or speaking it into being; it is the success and quality of life we experience when we are walking within God's will and living our lives in a way that pleases Him. So to become more successful and to thrive in our ventures, we must first align those ventures with God's desires.

God designed us with free will, and the will of mankind is strong. Each of us has things we would love to do or attain, from life experiences to material things and more. But just because we want something very badly doesn't mean it would be to our benefit to have it, or that our desiring it is in line with God's plans and purposes.

In order to prosper in this life, we need a combination of wisdom in how we steward our gifts, talents, thoughts, and material resources, and willingness to define prosperity not by having what *we* want, but by prioritizing the things of God.

When we are using our God-given talents and abilities to further His purposes and shape our lives to the praise of His glory, He is faithful to prosper us, as He has proved many times throughout human history.

TAKE ACTION:

What is your perspective on prosperity? Do you think it's in alignment with God's view? If not, how can you change your perspective?

WEALTH

IT'S TIME TO TALK ABOUT WEALTH—a subject that can be very touchy these days, particularly for younger generations.

It's often hard to relate to wealth, money, and possessions in a healthy way—especially for Christians! To some denominations it's sinful to have anything more than the bare minimum to live off of;

all else should be given to the needy. On the other hand, some Christians believe wealth is an indicator of God's favor—or that the more you have, the more you can help others.

Something I've had to learn is the issue isn't actually about money, because no one will ever be able to settle on what's the baseline number for too much or too little. It's all about the heart.

Think about it this way: God calls it grievous evil when wealth is hoarded to the harm of its owner. However, not everyone who's ever served God was penniless or without property or possessions. So if you're one who struggles with the subject of Christians and wealth, I offer this:

If anything in the whole world becomes enshrined on a person's heart to the point where it becomes their god, the thing they'd do anything to have or maintain—including wealth—then it is a grievous evil. Period.

To have wealth is not a sin; but to seek to possess it above all else, including the things God calls truly valuable—like wisdom!—and to cheat, lie, steal, or otherwise gain it in dishonorable ways that contradict the Word of God, *that* is sin.

Always remember that the appearance of a thing like wealth is not the metric by which God judges; it is the heart He weighs. And so must we.

What is Wealth?

When Scripture talks about wealth—particularly to caution us about the potential dangers of our attitude toward it—this is not always just a dollars-and-cents issue.

To be clear, the Bible never says that it's wrong to be wealthy. There were many people, rich by the standards of their time, who diligently followed God—like Abraham, Jacob, Paul's patroness Phoebe (who likely helped fund his travels), Boaz, Kings Solomon and David, etc. The acquisition of wealth is not sinful or wrong in God's eyes as long as it is done by just and honest means.

But even then, people must be careful not to put riches on a throne in their hearts such that acquiring or maintaining them becomes paramount to doing the will of God.

Jesus warned against this kind of worship of wealth when he said that "no servant is able to serve two lords, for either he will hate the one and love the other, or else he will be devoted to the one and think little of the other. You are not able to serve God and Wealth." (Luke 16:13)

What Does the Bible Say About Money/Wealth?

Ecclesiastes 5:10 - Whoever loves **money** never has enough; whoever loves **wealth** is never satisfied with their income. This too is meaningless.

Hebrews 13:5 - Keep your lives free from the love of **money** and be content with what you have, because God has said, "Never will I leave you; never will I forsake you."

1 Timothy 6:10 - For the love of **money** is a root of all kinds of evil, which some, reaching out for *it*, have been led astray from the faith and have pierced themselves through with many sorrows.

How Do I Relate to Wealth in a Healthy Way?

Remember that wealth is a means, not an end. It is not our security, sanctuary, or provision. God is all those things and more, and while He may bless us with financial welfare, that is not permission to reverse the roles of wealth and God in our lives.

That being the case, we should never be afraid to part with money if that's what God calls us to do. If He moves us to sow into others, give to a church or ministry, support an impoverished family, or even give up a comfortable lifestyle to do His work, our grip on our wealth and comfort can't be so tight that we refuse. That's the kind of unhealthy mindset we are warned against.

We must always hold wealth in balance: to be thankful for it but never rely on it to be our sufficiency. This is an important part of keeping our hearts free of idols and open to God's calling.

TAKE ACTION:

Do you find your focus is on gathering or maintaining your wealth rather than pursuing the things of God? Take time to meditate on God's heart concerning money so you can bring your focus into alignment with His!

PRAYER

IS PRAYER REALLY THAT IMPORTANT?
There's no shortage of resources debating the effectiveness and purpose of prayer, whether it has current application in Christian life or whether it falls on deaf ears. Some people say prayer should be a conversation and others say it's a one-sided petition

and anything you "hear back" is just a voice in your head.

I'm just here to share my own personal experience with prayer, which is that the more I do it, the easier it becomes and the closer I feel to God. I'm one of those who *has* experienced the voice of God when I pray to Him, so much so that it does feel conversational. Moreso than being zapped with revelation, seeing mental pictures or having dreams, I've realized that an active prayer life is how God and I communicate most clearly with each other. When I take time to focus on praying without distraction or disruption, my heart and the holy spirit within me are primed to receive instruction, edification, and guidance from Him.

To give some anecdotal evidence, I spent an entire month wrestling with a personal problem without lifting it up in prayer. I did a ton of things that normally help in these cases, yet it reaped no value. Finally, at the urging of several friends, I took a morning off from my usual routine and JUST sat in prayer about it. And within an hour, the floodgates opened and I felt the outpouring of God's provision over the situation. 24 hours later, my entire perspective on life and the situation in particular had completely shifted!

If you're one who questions whether prayer has any place in the modern Christian life, I invite you to put aside all else and ask what it could hurt to devote yourself to prayer. The very worst that happens is you pour your heart out to God—and maybe you "hear" nothing back.

But what if you do? What if a dedicated time of prayer is the last leap you need to cross a hurdle that's been in your path far too long? What if the key to a stronger, more intimate fellowship with your Creator is the humbleness required of you to prioritize your prayer life?

What if prayer IS all that important? Why *not* make it a priority and see for yourself?

WHAT IS PRAYER?

Merriam-Webster Dictionary defines **prayer** as "an address (such as a petition) to God or a god in word or thought."

Prayer is one of the most important aspects of Christian living. It's how we communicate with God and how we petition Him for help. It's one of the ways we express our gratitude, love, confusion, despair, hope, and grief to our Heavenly Father. Prayer also has a powerful effect on the spiritual climate around us.

When people pray against a spiritual attack, illness, or oppression over someone's life, this is often called "intercessory prayer," because prayer also allows us to intercede on the behalf of ourselves and others in situations beyond our mortal control. There are also methods of meditative or contemplative prayer, worshipful prayer, confessional prayer, and more!

The Bible tells us to pray often—without ceasing, in fact!—and to pray in different ways: alone and with others, aloud and silently, with words and in the spirit. Prayer is one thing that Christians from all walks of life and from every different denomination can do for one another.

We shouldn't be afraid to intercede on behalf of our brothers and sisters in Christ, no matter what, because God always hears our prayers—whether we speak eloquently or not.

What Does the Bible Say About Prayer?

1 Thessalonians 5:16-18 - Rejoice always, **pray** continually, give thanks in all circumstances; for this is God's will for you in Christ Jesus.

Colossians 5:2 - Devote yourselves to **prayer**, being watchful and thankful.

Hebrews 4:16 - Let us then approach God's throne of grace with confidence, so that we may receive mercy and find grace to help us in our time of need.

How Can I Become More Devoted to Prayer?

Devoting ourselves to prayer is easier or harder in different phases of life. Learning to pray constantly is not something most people become good at overnight, either!

Remember that prayer does not have to sound a certain way, or last a certain length, or include certain "keywords" to make it work. God knows you and how YOU speak, and He wants to hear from your heart!

Here are some ways to help make prayer a habit:

1) Roll it into your daily life. Take a look at the things you do throughout the day, such as reading emails, scrolling social media, or watching the news and search for how they create opportunities to pray!

2) Carve out time from your usual schedule to devote to focused prayer. This means shutting off your phone, turning off your music,

putting your book aside, and concentrating on nothing but being in the moment with God and Jesus, free from distractions.

3) Grab a prayer buddy. Find someone you can pray for and who will pray for you, and make sure you check in with each other throughout the day/week. Pray for each other out loud together when possible, and add their prayer needs to your dedicated prayer time each day.

4) Start a prayer board. Whether this is a note on your phone, a corkboard on your wall, a document in your office—whatever method works for you! Have prayer requests written down in one place where you can remember them, then pray through them frequently.

5) Join a prayer chain. Many different ministries have an email list you can join where prayer requests are mailed out, and pausing to pray for the requests as soon as they hit your inbox is great training toward making prayer a priority.

6) End the day with a prayer. Once you're in bed, the distractions start to fade away. Take some

time to thank God for the day, lift up your cares to Him, and release all your burdens into His hands.

Prayer is a habit-forming practice; the more we do it, the more conscious we become to repeat it. Eventually, it's second-nature to start praying when something comes to our attention; we will be bolder to approach God with our petitions; and as a result, we grow into stronger, more peaceful, and more courageous Christians.

TAKE ACTION:

Ask a friend, family member, coworker, etc. how you can pray for them. Make a conscious effort to lift the matter in prayer at least three times every day this week.

PRAISE

"GOD IS SO GOOD!" A phrase plastered on bathroom plaques and above-the-kitchen-table metal signs; but how often do we really take the time to say this *to God*?

Before conversational prayer really became a part of my life, it always felt a little strange to "praise God" in the sense of acknowledging aloud what He has done for me. The words tended to emerge too formal, stiff, and awkward; they sounded scripted, like a list of achievements read off at a graduation ceremony.

Yet over time and as life experience happens, and as I get to know my Maker on a more personal basis day by day, something has begun to work in my heart more heavily; similar to how I am with my friends, the "encourager of the group," I'm beginning to shift the tone of my conversations with God. Rather than listing off quick thanks and requests, I want to dive deeper into accolades. I want to speak to God like I would a friend, with my wholehearted belief, sincere gratitude and adoration, and deep trust and love.

When "praise" and "worship" are bundled together too closely, we risk losing the beauty of time taken specifically to express our love of the Father for all He is, all He has done, and all He will do. Does God know how amazing He is? Yes, I imagine He does! But there's a deep strengthening of the bond between us when we take time to acknowledge with our own lips, our own minds, our own hearts just how MUCH we love Him and are grateful for all He has done.

Yes, our God IS good. Let's make sure we take time to tell Him so, from the bottom of our heart!

WHAT IS PRAISE?

Merriam-Webster Dictionary defines "**praise**" as "to express favorable judgment of [something]; to glorify, especially by the attributes of perfection."

While the terms "praise" and "worship" are often used interchangeably or harmoniously, they are actually very different aspects of our interaction and relationship with God that call to and come from different parts of our spirit.

Praise is something we are called to do throughout the Bible because of what God has done for us and the world in general. Praise is the deserved and truthful acknowledgement of the righteous acts God has performed. In the same vein, we often praise (make truthful acknowledgement of) the achievements and actions of friends, family members, children, etc. Thus, when we praise God, what we're doing is giving glory to Him for all He is and has done, and especially to His attributes of perfection.

WHAT DOES THE BIBLE SAY ABOUT PRAISE?

Ephesians 1:5 - Let us **praise** God for his glorious grace, for the free gift he gave us in his dear Son!

Psalm 75:1 - We **praise** you, God, we **praise** you, for your Name is near; people tell of your wonderful deeds.

2 Corinthians 1:3 - **Praise** the God and Father of our Lord Jesus Christ! He is the Father who is compassionate and the God who gives comfort.

How Should I Praise God?

We are told many times, especially through the Psalms, to give praise to God for all He has done. Some of the ways we can praise God are with singing, dancing, and with musical instruments. But we can also praise God when we pray, by simply taking the time to acknowledge His hand in our lives and His mighty attributes and deeds.

In addition, we can offer praise to God by the way we live our lives. The Bible calls us to live our lives "to the praise of God's glory," meaning that we praise Him with our conduct—and that by that same conduct we inspire others to praise Him.

In other words, we praise God through obedience to His calling on our lives, and through our obedience, we lead others to recognize and acknowledge His attributes of perfection.

TAKE ACTION:

Carve out time in your prayer life to include consciously praising God for all His mighty deeds and specifically for the wonderful things He has done in your life!

WORSHIP

CHRISTIAN YOUTH CAMP WAS AN unparalleled experience in my teen years. Blistering hot days, late nights, the inimitable taste of camp food, the iffy air-conditioning and the guarantee of at least one unforgettable new friendship or even a whirlwind summer romance every year.

But between the long hours of studying in the blacktop tents, the later years of shopwork, and the evening teachings and campfires, the part my friends and I always looked forward to the most at camp was the worship sessions.

You can picture the scene: anywhere from 50-80 teenagers piled into a gymnasium, the sour green light destroying any guess as to the hour outside. The older camp counselors are exhausted and the attendees are awkwardly shifting their feet and either clustering together or shuffling apart, still trying to figure out exactly where they fit within this extended family setting for the week. When the first song starts, it's usually "Dive" by Steven Curtis Chapman—a classic "get your blood pumping" opener—and by the end of the first chorus, the most outgoing and enthusiastic campers and councilors are on their feet, jumping in the aisle, or line-dancing at the foot of the stage.

Yet for every person who's up there, there's another handful hanging back. Public worship can be such a vulnerable thing, and for some it's harder to dance before the Lord than others. But the outgoing ones start to trickle back, grabbing their reluctant friends both old and new, dragging them up to the front. One by one, they forget to make it about them—they make it about God instead. The community feeling swells with the raised voices, the dancing feet. It's a glimpse of the worship David led in the streets with the Ark of the Covenant's return. It's maybe even a glimpse of eternity—we'll have to see when we get there.

Gradually, the songs start to wind down. It's always stuck in my head, that pattern—two upbeat songs, two slow ones, maybe just one more slow depending on what the worship team's been practicing, a setlist to prepare listeners for the segue into prayer and manifestations, then the teaching or study session afterward.

But during those last two songs, something remarkable happens.

See, there's this kid—every year, there's at least one. He's super cool, he's chill, he's a little above it all. He's only here because his parents made him go. He's spent most of the sessions doodling in his notebook and endured the teachings staring into space. It's easy to make assumptions about this boy, about who he is and what he's going to get out of this week.

And then the last songs start; and suddenly this kid who no one was quite sure how to reach, we realize God knew *exactly* how to reach him. By the end of the final verse he's down on his knees between the chairs in the last row where he tucked himself away during the upbeat songs; his head is bowed, and he weeps.

It's the silent, heavy sobs of the heart touched by God, and all around him, the kids who didn't mesh with him before, the ones who were either too cool like him to show it or not cool enough, gather around. Their hands are on his shoulders. Quiet prayer starts. Assurances and hugs and words of comfort and love crowd out the awkwardness.

In the turn of a moment, the act of worship pulls out the truth of that boy from the mask he wore into the room. And he sees his Creator. And he feels seen.

There's a lot that can be said on the subject of worship, but when I think about this word, it always comes back to the sinner in all of us, broken and stripped bare, laid out at the feet of Jesus. I see in the love songs we sing to God a profound prayer that connects us all, heart-to-heart, straight back to Him.

On humid summer mornings when I sit on my front porch—grown now, married to one of those background kids I dragged with me to the front during "Dive", and now with a kiddo of our own—sometimes I close my eyes and I still feel all those threads connecting us in reverence and love to the Creator of us all.

That, my friends, is what worship is to me.

What is Worship?

Merriam-Webster Dictionary defines **worship** as "to honor or show reverence for a divine being or supernatural power; to regard with great or extravagant respect, honor, or devotion."

Whereas praise is something we are called to do, and *can* do regardless of how we feel because it is an acknowledgement of the simple fact of God's mighty works, worship is rooted in a deep sense of devotion and adoration that comes from deep within us. It involves a wholehearted submission of self so that we become filled with nothing but adoration and honor for our God.

We see this play out often in powerful worship sessions, both congregationally and privately, where someone might fall to their knees, bow their head, lift their hands, sing at the top of their voice, etc. These are all acts of surrender in which we open ourselves absolutely to the expression of worship, making the moment not about us, but about being in relationship with Him.

Ultimately, worship is a heart-posture of reverence and surrender before God.

What Does the Bible Say About Worship?

John 4:24 - God is spirit, and those who **worship** him must **worship** in spirit and truth.

Psalm 95:6 - Come, let us bow down in **worship**, let us kneel before the Lord our Maker.

Romans 12:1 - I appeal to you therefore, brothers, by the mercies of God, to present your bodies as a living sacrifice, holy and acceptable to God, which is your spiritual **worship**.

How Can I Become More Worshipful?

Like many spiritual actions, becoming more worshipful often requires carving out dedicated time from our busy lives to prioritize the things of God. With worship, this may look like setting aside time for practices that help you enter into a state of worship.

Many people find that music is a key factor for worship; the right song can bring them into a state of wholehearted, self-surrendered worship at the feet of Jesus. Because musical tastes differ so widely, it's up to the individual to find what songs, if any, are "worship songs" for them.

There is also an aspect of worship in how we live our lives, similar to praise. When we operate from a state of devoted submission to God, it changes how we walk out our day-to-day lives. Scripture tells us that the saved will worship God for eternity, but this isn't indicative of a future spent singing and dancing forever. We will live lives much like the ones we have now—working and playing and being a family together, as God intended it from the beginning—but with all the chaos and sin removed from the picture. So that means we will worship God through our work and play and way of being then, and we can do the same thing now!

When we are mindful of the things that glorify and honor God, and when the posture of our hearts is that of complete dedication to Him, we can lay down our love of self and elevate Him above all else, living as sacrifices, as the Book of Romans tells us. In this way, we worship Him with our very way of being—with Him, with the people around us, and in our personal lives.

TAKE ACTION:

Make space this week for at least fifteen minutes of undivided worship time, just you and God—no distractions! Then see if you can make this fifteen minutes a daily practice.

WORTHINESS

"I CAN'T BELIEVE YOU WOULD do that for me!"

If you numbered the times this phrase or something like it has come out of my mouth, it would be an inordinate sum. For as long as I can remember, I've struggled with feelings of inadequacy and low self-worth and self-esteem. I know I'm not alone in this; it can be difficult to grasp our worth through the eyes of those who show us kindness. How much moreso worthiness in the eyes of a perfect God?

One of my goals for many years has been to accept the worthiness God has placed within me as a being created in His image. This requires dismantling decades where I've been measuring my worth based on the world's standards and found myself lacking. I know I will never be perfect, but there is worth in me because I am a child of God, made in His likeness for good works. What a blessing that is!

Instead of "I can't believe Jesus did that for me," I'm trying to shift my thinking to "Thank you for deeming me worthy of that sacrifice, Jesus. I'm going to live my life as best I can to make the most of what you gave for me!" Instead of rejecting the gift God placed in me because I'm "not as good as others," I'm turning my focus to fulfilling the purpose for which He created me. And instead of dwelling on all my unworthiness, I'm keeping my eyes on the One who gave His Son, and the Son who laid down his life, so that people like me could be part of a family.

We indeed have worth. The Creator Who made us decrees it. And who are we to claim we know better than Him about our true value?

Thank you, Jesus, for deeming us all worthy of that sacrifice!

What is Worthiness?

Merriam-Webster Dictionary defines **worthiness** as "having worth or excellence; enough worth or excellence; sufficient worth or excellence."

Most of us spend our entire lives fighting to feel worthy. Whether by a wound dealt to us in childhood or by the simple result of living in a broken world that has more time and attention to pay to some than others, by the time many people reach adulthood they have struggled with feelings of doubt surrounding their worth...sometimes for years.

It is ultimately impossible to experience our intrinsic value or worth when the source we draw from is our appeal to the world or even ourselves. In some way or another, we will always fall short of having "sufficient" worth for this world due to its fallen nature and the ever-shifting climate of its affections.

For that reason, our sense and definition of our own worth should not come from the world's opinion of us, but from what God says of us.

What Does the Bible Say About Our Worth?

Romans 5:8 - But God shows his love for us in that while we were still sinners, Christ died for us.

Ephesians 2:8-9 - For by grace you have been saved through faith. And this is not your own doing; it is the gift of God.

Luke 12:7 - Why, even the hairs of your head are all numbered. Fear not; you are of more value than many sparrows.

How Should I Approach My Worth?

There are two primary ways to handle the matter of your worth. The first is to find the places in your life where you measure your value against what the world deems worthy—wealth, fame, sensuality, wits, smarts, etc.—and turn those over to God instead. Let *His* truth and *His* scale of worthiness become the one you measure yourself upon.

We are made in the image of God. He formed us in our mothers' wombs. Apart from His vision of us, there is no truly accurate measure of our worth. So we must learn to make His standard the one we hold ourselves to, and to embrace the inherent worthiness we have as His creations, fearfully and wonderfully made.

The second way is to realize that ultimately, it is not about us. This is not to say we negate our intrinsic value—God certainly didn't when He gave His only Son to redeem us! But the pursuit of our worth should not become the focal point of our lives.

One of the great purposes God sees in His children is that we serve our worthy King, Jesus. So in order to not be swept up in matters of self-worth to the point where we obsess over our value, we must recognize that we were worthy of being bought and paid for by the Blood of the Lamb. Now we serve him above all else, even above the pursuit of measuring our own worth, for *he* is worthy above all else of our praise, love, and sacrifice.

TAKE ACTION:

Do you tend to base your sense of worth on how the world sees you, or how God sees you? Meditate on what Scripture says about your worth and pray that God will give you eyes to see yourself as He does.

FUNCTION

"*I DON'T CARE WHAT YOUR* role in the ministry is. What is your function?"

The first time someone asked me this, I blanked out. The mashup of "receptionist, shipping department head, writer, and editor" died on my tongue. Suddenly I was in sixth grade again, frozen mute in my chair because I forgot to mentally practice saying "here" sixty-five times before the teacher called on me.

It was winter of 2018 the first time I realized my function in the Body of Christ and the role I served as a worker in ministry were not the same thing. By the end of that day, I had a new answer—one that utterly reset a lifelong vision, reassembled my goals, and in the years that followed, opened countless doors to places I had never once dreamed I'd walk.

All because I realized what my function was.

Recognizing the purpose for which you were created is a powerful thing—just read the Book of Esther and how Esther's realization of her purpose shaped the future for the people of God! Within Christianity, there tends to be a narrow view of valuable functions, an outlook which was at least partially responsible for why I didn't recognize *my* function for what it was in the first quarter-century of my life.

But there's a tremendous shift happening in many Christian circles now; a recognition of called artists, musicians, writers, social workers, gardeners, farmers, schoolteachers, social media moguls, bakers, scientists—you name a field, God is calling His workers to sow Truth there. And a harvest is being reaped, my friends. The longer I live in my function, the more I see it firsthand.

God has called more than apostles, prophets, evangelists, pastors and teachers—at least in the sense we're used to thinking of them. Look beyond the pulpits and outreach of organized religion; look at the passion that burns within you, the fire God has lit in your heart. The one you've maybe never fully stoked, but it makes everything within you come alive in zeal and urgency—it makes you feel closer than ever to the One who created that flame within you.

Now answer this: what's YOUR function?

WHAT IS FUNCTION?

Merriam-Webster Dictionary defines **function** as "the action for which a person or thing is specially fitted or used or for which a thing exists; purpose."

Each of us was created on purpose, for a purpose. We are equipped with a function or functions with which we serve God and Jesus, our families, the Body of Christ, and the world at large. The more I've become aware of the importance of a person fulfilling their function, the more I've realized how often it looks like answering a calling God has placed within the individual's spirit.

Many people have spent years fulfilling the function God designed them for without even realizing that's what they were doing! Writers writing, teachers teaching, mediators mediating, servants serving, and on and on.

WHAT DOES THE BIBLE SAY ABOUT FUNCTION?

Romans 12:4 - For just as we have many members in one body and all the members do not have the same **function**...

1 Corinthians 12:6 – There are varieties of **effects**, but the same God who works all things in all persons.

Ephesians 4:15-16 - But speaking the truth in love, we are to grow up in every way into him who is the head, Christ, from whom the whole body, being fitted together and held together by every supporting ligament, with each individual part doing *its* proper **function**, produces the growth of the body with the goal of building itself up in love.

HOW CAN I FULFILL MY FUNCTION?

Another way to look at function is this: it's the assignment God has given us to carry out, each one as individuals. So you fulfill your function by carrying out your assignment; and even if two people have the same assignment, they may not carry it out the same way. God might call one person to teach scholars and another to teach children, and in His eyes both are equally important.

Discovering your function often takes a lot of introspection and prayer; but it can also be as simple as looking for patterns in your life where God has nudged you, or where you've felt drawn to certain things—like to design, or to make music, or to encourage or research or evangelize or to pastor or serve.

Once you know what your function is, it's as simple and as difficult as having the boldness to walk out in it regardless of what people think or say. There will always be some who elevate one function over another or say certain assignments from God are of greater value or importance than others. That's human nature, folks!

But the truth is, God assigns functions because in His eyes they are *all valuable*. They, and we who have them, all serve a unique purpose in the Body of Christ. We must embrace our purpose, our function, our calling, our assignment—and then get busy doing it, staying in sync with God to be certain we are walking out our function according to His will.

TAKE ACTION:

Do you know your function in the Body of Christ? If so, what can you do to get busy doing your function? If not, take some time in prayer and ask God to reveal what His assignment is for you!

CALLING

ON THE SURFACE, FUNCTION and calling can look awfully similar. I tend to fall back on my own experience to elucidate the difference: my function in the Body of Christ is *writing*. I've spent decades honing this craft, but I also recognize a God-given understanding of language and communication placed within me. This is my function.

My *calling*, on the other hand, is to write within two very specific spheres: Christian encouragement and secular fiction.

So, to use some more well-known examples, someone's *function* may be as an evangelist, but is their *calling* to inner-city kids or people of a foreign nation? Is God calling the teacher to teach Christians or teach unbelievers? Is the pastor meant to council struggling couples or recovering addicts?

Isn't that a cool distinction? Recognizing your function equips you for God's work; understanding your calling dispatches you to carry it out.

We are all looking for places where we can carry out the great commission and make disciples; some are making disciples of new believers, others are convicting the saved to start living the *disciplined life*. The wonderful thing is that God knows each of His children so personally; He has and *will* empower you to carry out the mission He's assigned you to.

Once we understand our function, it's time to ardently pursue God's heart for where and how He wants us to make use of it! What an exciting and enthralling opportunity to be at work with our Heavenly Father!

What is A Calling?

Merriam-Webster Dictionary defines **calling** as "a strong inner impulse toward a particular course of action, especially when accompanied by conviction of divine influence."

It's common to hear Christians talk about the calling they feel God has placed on their life. Some feel called to missions overseas, some to work with the abused or battered or downtrodden in their area, some to evangelize or preach or teach, etc.

While some of us may feel called to *specific* "mission fields", tasks, etc., as a whole the Body of Christ has a calling on it, a commission to make disciples and to do our part as living epistles, representing God and Jesus to the world.

What Does the Bible Say About Calling?

Ephesians 4:1 - Therefore I, the prisoner of the Lord, urge you to walk in a manner worthy of the **calling** with which you were **called**.

Galatians 5:13 - For you, brothers *and sisters*, were **called** to freedom; only do not *use* the freedom for an opportunity to *indulge* the flesh, but through love serve one another.

Colossians 3:15 - And let the peace of Christ be the umpire in your hearts, for indeed you were **called** as one body to this *peace*; and *always* be thankful!

How Do I Find My Calling?

As we've noted, a person's calling often walks hand-in-hand with their function, because God has equipped us for what He is calling us to do.

We can also find our calling by being attentive to the places where we feel the holy spirit pressing in on our lives. Our natural sympathies, interests, and inclinations often point down the road toward what we are being called to do. The beautiful thing about being in relationship with God is that He will also train us up in what we need to do as we step forward into our calling.

But there is also the broader calling for the Body of Christ which we should all be answering on a daily basis: to walk in love, to bring Christ to people by our actions and behavior, to encourage, uplift, and be peacemakers, to speak the truth in love and to be such good witnesses and disciples of Christ that we inspire others to do the same.

In other words, if you don't know or don't yet feel what the calling of God is on your life, don't wait to find out! Get busy doing the work of the Lord right where you are. This is pleasing to God regardless of whether you ever feel the urge to partake in missions or answer any other sort of calling.

TAKE ACTION:

Take a step this week to move forward in either the personal or corporate calling of the Lord on your life!

GRACE

"WHY SHOULD GOD CARE ABOUT me when I'm just...me?"

Have you ever found yourself wondering this, or heard it from the lips of someone you know?

Barring those with a seared conscience who can't hear the voice of reason no matter what, I think *most* of us have an inherent sense that we are fallen. This doesn't amount to us walking around hating ourselves, it simply means we're aware that we fall short. The price of being a fallen race living in a fallen world.

But think about this: Scripture doesn't say "but mankind was so fantastic and righteous and awesome, God sent His only son..."

No. "For *God so loved.*"

That love hasn't expired, you know? People were no more righteous or deserving of divine favor back then than we are now; in fact, arguably, we were further from God than ever at the time, as the blood of Jesus hadn't yet paid the price for sins. Yet what remains eternal before, during, and after the life of Jesus is God's love, and through that love, His grace—first the grace that He gave His Son, and now the grace that even though we are all *just me*, He is invested, concerned, and at work in our lives as much as we will invite Him in.

How do we react to grace? I ask myself this often, but I think I'm finally coming to understand it:

1. I have to stop trying to deserve it (never going to happen)
2. I have to stop telling God I shouldn't have it (He gets to make that call, not me)

3. I have to start being thankful for it (stop waiting for the shoe to drop)
4. I have to pay it forward—as I've been given grace, grace should I give (the REALLY hard one).

WHAT IS GRACE?

Merriam-Webster Dictionary defines grace as "unmerited divine assistance given to humans for their regeneration or sanctification." Biblically, grace is often spoken of in tandem with peace, because the divine assistance of God that comes regardless of how far short we fall is a great comfort to so many!

Grace is a cornerstone principle in the Christian's relationships with God and one another, because we are all part of God's family by grace through our acceptance of Jesus as our Lord. In return, we show grace to others, knowing we are all equally undeserving and yet equally sanctified by the blood of Jesus, and thus all equal members of his Body.

WHAT DOES THE BIBLE SAY ABOUT GRACE?

Ephesians 2:8 - For by **grace** you have been saved through trust, and this is not from yourselves, *it is* the gift of God.

Romans 3:24 - *but* [all] are declared righteous freely by his **grace** through the redemption that is *accomplished* in Christ Jesus

2 Thessalonians 2:16-17: Now may our Lord Jesus Christ himself, and God our Father, who loved us and by **grace** gave us Age-abiding encouragement and a good hope, encourage and establish your hearts in every good work and word.

Colossians 4:6 - Let your speech always be with **grace**, seasoned with salt, so that you come to know how you must respond to each one.

How Can I Become More Gracious?

One of the greatest grace-builders in our lives is when we recognize the grace that has been given to us and how we are called to "pay it forward". None of us deserves God's grace; none of us deserves to be in God's family on our own merit. Yet when we were still dead in our sins, God gave His Son for us, and He opened the door for us to come into his family. You have been given that grace; rather than bragging about how we deserved it, we should all focus on ensuring as many people as possible are saved through that grace, too!

In the Parable of the Unforgiving Servant, Jesus warns against a refusal to forgive (show grace) to others when we ourselves have been forgiven of much. Graciousness has its roots in recognizing what God has lavished on us—grace upon grace—and striving to spread the life-changing message and benefits of that grace to those around us.

When you struggle to be gracious toward other people, remember the grace that was shown to you; and then step forward to live out that same grace in how you deal with them.

TAKE ACTION:

Is there a place in your life where you could give more grace to someone—even yourself? How would the abundant grace of God exemplify the way forward in this situation?

SALVATION

SO MUCH HAS BEEN SAID, debated, discussed, fought over and—**checks Thesaurus**—pettifogged about Christian salvation, it's become something of a laughingstock for those outside the faith.

It's rare to find a Christian who hasn't argued the finer points and potentials of salvation—I myself can't cry innocent on that! But when it comes down to it, I think sometimes we get so wrapped up in arguing the details and deliberates of salvation, we lose sight of the word *itself* and its implication.

Salvation. From Latin root "*salvare*", to save. For something to be saved, there must be something *from which* it is saved.

Do you ever think we get so caught up in arguing for our particular view on salvation that we forget to stop and simply bask in the awestriking wonder, the humbling breadth of what we have been saved *from*? Of the sacrifice that brought this salvation about?

Sometimes amidst pondering the particulars of salvation, how *exactly* it came about, whether it's permanent or loseable or forfeitable, I think we forget to fall on our knees and simply thank God and Jesus for their joint sacrifice—the Father giving His only Son, the Son giving his very life—to secure that salvation for us.

Sometimes it just hits me, out of nowhere, what I have been saved from eternally by Jesus's sacrifice; then it occurs to me to wonder what trust and faith and co-laboring with God has saved me from in *this* life, likely things I will never know of until I see the tapestry of my years laid out before me in God's presence.

Just—WOW. No doubt the details of salvation are important, but equally as powerful is the sheer reality of everything that word entails. Brothers and sisters, we have been *saved* from something, our lives redeemed; as one Dictionary says, we have been "[saved] or [protected] from harm, risk, loss, destruction, etc."

Sure, we will face struggles, even harm, risk, loss, and destruction in his life; but those things can't keep us down forever like they would have had we not accepted Jesus as Lord...because those who trust in him have been, are, and will ultimately be, saved.

What a powerful reality. Praise God!

WHAT IS SALVATION?

Merriam-Webster Dictionary defines **salvation** as "deliverance from the power and effects of sin." The only means of true and everlasting deliverance from the consequences of sin is through belief in Jesus Christ.

While the culmination of our salvation is still future—in the sense that we will (likely) still die in this life before the Lord's return—it's also a present reality as well because it's sealed up with God from the moment we make Jesus our Lord, until that future time.

While salvation does not guarantee anyone an easy life, it does guarantee us life in a coming age that will be absolutely perfect. This is made possible because when a person makes Jesus Lord in their life—submitting to his leadership and will—and truly believes in the depths of their heart that he died and was raised from the dead, they are also claiming that death as payment for the sins they will inevitably commit in this life.

The only other alternative is for the individual to deny that payment, in other words agreeing to pay for their sin with their own blood when Jesus judges the world—and God makes it very clear that the wages of sin is death.

This is why accepting Jesus as Lord is the only true path to salvation. While many other religions claim to have a path to Heaven, only the path through the remission of sins by submission to Jesus invokes the blood price needed to save our lives.

WHAT DOES THE BIBLE SAY ABOUT SALVATION?

Acts 4:12 - And in no one else [but Jesus] is there **salvation**, for there is no other name under heaven that has been given among people by which we must be **saved**.

Ephesians 1:13 - In whom you also, when you heard the word of truth—the good news of your **salvation**—and when you believed in him [Jesus], were sealed with the promised holy spirit...

Titus 2:11 - For the grace of God has appeared, bringing **salvation** to all people...

How Can I Be Saved?

Romans 10:9-10 tells us that if we confess with our mouths that Jesus is Lord (not just saying the words, but confessing him as our *personal* Lord—meaning that we surrender wholeheartedly to him and become his hands and feet, moving in submission to him) and believe in our hearts that God raised him from the dead, we will be saved. We've accepted his blood as the price for our sins. Now we step forward in that new reality.

The Bible tells us that the works of our lives will be evidence of this faith-based surrender to the Lordship of Christ. And from the moment we believe and are saved, we will start to see evidence of it: we can manifest the holy spirit within us through things like speaking in tongues, prophecy, receiving revelation, and performing miracles.

Many Christians, especially new ones, feel a sharp friction between the sin of their past and the new creation they've become. This should be heeded! It's part of God's spirit working within us to want to do, and to carry out, His will.

Another thing God wants for us is that we would not walk around wondering *if* we're even saved after we've confessed Jesus as Lord. God wants all men to be saved and come to a knowledge of truth; He is not looking for the first excuse to toss you out.

When you believe and confess, God will begin to work in you and *with you* to fulfill your glorious destiny as His child. This isn't a time for fear, but for learning and growing and for embracing the powerful new nature as you step into relationship with the Creator.

TAKE ACTION:

Is there someone you can share the beauty of the salvation message with – either a person who's not yet a believer, or a believer who needs a reminder of just how wonderful salvation is? Make it a point to strike up a conversation this week!

DESTINY

HAVING A DESTINY IS A HEAVY BURDEN.

When I think about destiny, it evokes a mental image of a straight path, one often dismal and dangerous, toward an ending that likely threatens death or pain. Now, maybe I've watched *The Empire Strikes Back* too many times, but somehow the words

"It is your *destiny*" don't give me the warm fuzzies. More like the heebie jeebies.

Thankfully, I don't suspect any of us carries a universe-saving, empire-crossing, inter-galactic destiny on our shoulders—at least not in the sense that it's up to us to save the world. In fact, the person with the most set and powerful destiny, like the kind we hear of in the epics, was Jesus. *He* carried the destiny of mankind's salvation all the way to the cross. He knew what he was getting into, but like any true hero, he took it upon himself anyway, setting captives loose with his shed blood.

And in his passing and resurrection, a new destiny was born.

What we have as followers of Jesus is not a destiny just the same as his; we do not each carry that weight on our shoulders, the burden of redeeming mankind. What we have is a destiny we can choose; a destiny not for *us*, but for a *group*, the Body of Christ.

Collectively, we all shoulder that responsibility together, and doesn't that just make it feel lighter? Not only that, but the destiny of God's family is not dismal, nor does it end in death or pain; instead it promises a glorious future.

The course of events, the *destiny* for those who choose God, who make Jesus their Lord, is clear:

everlasting life in utmost paradise. If you ask me, that's what I wanted to be destined for!

WHAT IS DESTINY?

Merriam-Webster Dictionary defines **destiny** as "something to which a person or thing is destined; a predetermined course of events often held to be an irresistible power or agency."

The subject of destiny is tricky when it comes to Scripture because it doesn't mesh very well with the notion of free will. Do we have a destiny in the sense that from the time we're born, the steps of our lives are determined for us? That's not the design most easily determined from the world around us, or from God's interaction with man.

Rather than an irresistible power holding our lives to a specific outcome, what we have are individual callings within a greater destiny—which is the glorious future that the Body of Christ as an entity is destined for, regardless of which individuals choose to be in or out of it.

WHAT DOES THE BIBLE SAY ABOUT DESTINY?

Ephesians 1:11 - In whom we also were claimed as *God's* possession, having been **decided upon in**

advance according to the purpose of the one who is working all things according to the plan of his will...

Romans 8:30 - And those whom he **decided in advance**, these he also called, and those whom he called, these he also declared righteous, and those whom he declared righteous, these he also glorified.

WHAT IS MY DESTINY?

As a member of the Body of Christ, saved by your confession and belief, you are destined to everlasting life in eternity. You are destined for a place in Christ's kingdom. This is the power of your identity in Christ, and while it doesn't decide your every step in life from here to the end, it should absolutely shape the path you *choose.*

The Bible talks in certain places about predestination, which refers not the individual's destiny but to the broader destiny of creation: that salvation would come through Jesus Christ. Once we submit to him as our Lord, our destiny is to be with him forever.

Knowing that is our destiny, we can all become emboldened to walk in the power of that mighty and secure future, keenly aware that we are a part of a glorious destiny: to be redeemed along with the rest of creation when Jesus comes to restore all things as they should be.

TAKE ACTION:

Take time this week to recognize and embrace your God-given destiny as a member of His Church—then seek out ways to bring others into this glorious destination as well!

COMPASSION

IN 2020, MUCH OF THE world experienced an unprecedented global pandemic. All arguments as to the severity aside, there were economic, mental, emotional, and non-viral physical impacts that could be ignored. Very few were uncompromised by one or more of the above fallouts.

Each week brought fresh challenges. Constant debates flew back and forth; judgement against those who sanitized everything and wouldn't leave their houses, judgement against those who declined the use of face masks, judgement against the shoppers standing only six feet apart and those who won't go down an aisle if someone else is there. Judgement against those complying with guidelines and judgement against those exercising the freedom not to.

While having a conversation with friends about the often-polarizing responses to the pandemic, it began weighing heavy on my heart how God would have me relate to my fellow humans at that time. What would have the greatest impact, the most positive effect on my sanity, without adding to the burden of judgement so broadly cast?

What came to me was *compassion*.

Compassion is as desperately needed in these days as it was when Jesus saw the people at the shore like lost sheep without a shepherd. So many feel lost, uncertain, and angry, and everyone reacts to this differently. But across the spectrum, the one thing everyone could use is a whole heap of compassion; for us to recognize that others' reactions by and large may come from the same place as ours.

We can have compassion because it means recognizing the discomfort, pain, or conviction that can be at the root of the action, whether we approve or not. Compassion allows us to see and minister to the heart of the person. Then we're much more capable of loving them like Jesus would. And that, more than *anything else*, is what we all need today.

What is Compassion?

Merriam-Webster Dictionary defines **compassion** as "sympathetic consciousness of others' distress together with a desire to alleviate it."

It's in this desire to alleviate the distress of others that compassion differs from similar feelings like pity and sympathy. Compassion is more visceral in some ways; it is not just a feeling-word, it is an *action-word*. More than acknowledging pain, compassion desires to lighten the load.

As Christians, we are not only called to have compassion on others; we are called to *act* on that compassion. We are equipped in many ways to do that: with truth, prayer, through giving of our means—which can be time, money, prayer, or a number of other things—through manifestations of the holy spirit to offer comfort and encouragement, and so much more.

Not only are we called to be compassionate, but it's important to recognize that God also has compassion on *us* (Lam. 3:22-23). Our Heavenly Father has sympathetic consciousness of our distress, with a desire to alleviate it! Not only is that a reason to celebrate how we are known and loved and *seen* by our Creator, it also empowers us to come before His Throne of Grace with petitions in our hour of need, knowing it is the desire of His heart to meet those needs.

What Does the Bible Say About Compassion?

Ephesians 4:32 - Be kind and **compassionate** to one another, forgiving each other, just as in Christ God forgave you.

1 Peter 3:8 - Finally, all of you, be like-minded, be sympathetic, love one another, be **compassionate** and humble.

Lamentations 3:22-23 - Because of the Lord's great love we are not consumed, for his **compassions** never fail. They are new every morning; great is your faithfulness.

How Can I Become More Compassionate?

One of the best steps toward growing our capacity for compassion is to recognize the intrinsic value of our fellow humans in God's eyes. Everyone was created by Him, and He would love to see every single person in the world become saved and gain a knowledge of the truth; because in addition to securing their future for everlasting life, that truth will set them free from all kinds of struggle and suffering in *this* life—many of the distresses that threaten to cripple them.

When we begin to see people's value through God's eyes rather than by the measure of our own standard, our sympathetic consciousness of their needs and the urge to help meet those needs becomes a natural outworking. From there, we enter into the question of how to walk out that compassion.

TAKE ACTION:

Do you find you lack compassion toward others? Do you think you are seeing them through God's eyes? If not, ask God to help you shift your perspective, beginning today!

MERCY

THIS MAY SOUND WEIRD, but I love showing mercy. There is just something in my mental and emotional wiring that has a deep appreciation for the powerful effect mercy has on others. I guess I see it like this: there are few things that are a better witness of the redeeming love of Jesus than when we choose compassion and mercy where retributive justice would be possible, especially when the other person is fully aware of that possibility.

I see it this way because I've experienced it; growing up, from broken valuables to missed deadlines to sharp words and outbursts, I gave my mom *more* than her share of opportunities to be merciful toward me. One incident stands out—more clearly for her than me—yet in knowing it, I realize how this one moment shaped my entire viewpoint on mercy...the way I see it and how I show it.

As my mom tells it:

After a particularly long day, the dinner dishes were done and the kitchen was finally cleaned up. It was time for you kids to finish your chocolate milk, brush teeth and settle in for bed. For some reason, you took the lid off your sippy cup and were frantically trying to get it back on before I rounded the corner – and it slipped! There was chocolate milk everywhere – cabinets, stove, countertops, floor, walls – nothing escaped.

In the split second between my formulating something about how you're not to take the lid off your sippy cup and deciding how many beanie babies would be quarantined and for how long, I was interrupted. What came out of my mouth instead was, "WOOPS! Good thing we have more Hersheys!"

You kinda looked at me puzzled, but I remember we laughed together about it and you helped with recon while you finished your second chocolate milk.

This incident was textbook of the model of mercy my mom showed me growing up. Her discipline operated from a place of love, whether I received punishment or mercy; and I always remember that as hard as it was to 'fess up when I did wrong, there were so many times I received mercy where I could've just as easily had my beanie babies put in quarantine—or worse!
This has shaped my whole worldview, honestly. It's made me default to mercy when I'm faced with being wronged, because I know the relief, the sense of love, and the deep urge to do better, be better, and grow as a person that comes from realizing you've been given a second chance.
When people ask why God would be merciful to sinners, I often think of the lesson my mother's love taught me: that rather than seeking to take advantage of her mercy when I was in the wrong, that mercy

made me yearn to become the best version of myself. I thoroughly and unequivocally trusted the love behind her mercy and wanted to live a life deserving of it.

So it should be with us and God. This is what I mean by the witness of mercy, why it is so valuable that we keep a healthy perspective on our offenses and what we are owed when someone wrongs us.

When we're willing to let go of a hurt or something due us, and show mercy to others, we are in that moment living a godly precedent, showing by our actions the very way our Creator is with us.

And what a powerful lesson that mercy can be.

WHAT IS MERCY?

Merriam-Webster Dictionary defines **mercy** as "compassion or forbearance shown especially to an offender or to one subject to one's power."

While grace and mercy are sometimes used interchangeably to convey God's relationship with us, they are actually very different things. Whereas *grace* is undeserved divine favor and involves the bountiful blessings God has lavished on us despite our many shortcomings, *mercy* is the way that God withholds the punishment we deserve for those shortcomings.

Grace and mercy *are* equal aspects of our relationship with God, however. He has mercy on us despite our sins, and in His grace, He goes above and beyond; not only does He show forbearance, He even blesses us and bestows gifts on us despite how we fall short!

What Does the Bible Say About Mercy?

Romans 11:30-31 - For just as at one time you defied God, but now have received **mercy** as a result of their disobedience, even so they too have now been disobedient, that by the **mercy** shown to you they also can now receive **mercy**.

2 Corinthians 4:1 - Therefore, since we have this ministry, just as we received **mercy**, we are not discouraged.

How Can I Become More Merciful?

Much like with grace, we give because He first gave to us. God has showed us mercy and we in turn should be merciful toward those who wrong or offend us—not seeking absolution for our own satisfaction, but extending the sort of mercy that reflects the nature of our God.

So in order to become more merciful, we first recognize our humble position and the mercy God has bestowed on us when we've sinned against Him; then we extend that same godly mercy to others who have wronged us, recognizing that there are times when a show of mercy does more for the Kingdom of Christ than retribution ever will.

Ultimately, the strength and maturity to be merciful rather than vengeful comes from a place of understanding our own status with God and recognizing that if He can forgive us for our shortcomings, <u>we can extend forbearance</u> and forgiveness to others, too.

TAKE ACTION:

Is there a situation in your life where you could afford to show mercy to someone who's wronged you? How will you go about being merciful this week?

SEXUALITY

SEXUALITY IS ONE OF THE most polarizing and hotly-debated topics, not just in Christianity, but throughout the world today. Many people choose whether or not to follow Jesus based on how Christianity addresses any number of sexual topics.

Why is this so important to mankind? Probably because God created us as sexual beings, with very innate urges. As if that wasn't enough, we are bombarded by everything from perfume ads to TV shows to pornography all aimed at stirring up sexual desires for the sake of views, clicks, and the all-powerful dollar.

Christianity seems to have two fairly polarized reactions to living in a sex-saturated era: silencing all talk of it until it becomes practically taboo, or treating it so lightly it runs rampant and unchecked within the church.

Neither response is right, of course; God doesn't want us ignorant about sexual matters or themes, but He wants us to honor the sanctity of the subject; not to treat it as a byword, a curse, or something we can dabble in lightly without repercussion.

Why is sex so important to God? It is a supernaturally binding, joining, captivating act that impacts a person on multiple levels including physical, emotional, mental, and spiritual. We may not even be aware of all the ways sexual acts impact us, but God is very clear: the bond that exists between two sexually-joined people does have ramifications, whether that is handled too lightly OR too heavily.

As Christians, we cannot afford to play loosely with the topic of sexuality, nor can we afford to run from it—and we serve no one by making it "off limits". It is a part of the Creator's design for us, and it was meant to be a gift handled with care and respect.

It's up to us to bring the healing light of that fact to a world that is, like it or not, sexually awakened.

WHAT IS SEXUALITY?

Merriam-Webster Dictionary defines **sexuality** as "the quality or state of being sexual; of, relating to, or associated with sex or the sexes."

"Sexuality" has also lately become a term for one's sexual preferences, but we'll stick to discussing the broader term of sexuality. God has plenty to say about the topic of sex, and it behooves anyone searching for sexual truth to explore the Scriptures themselves pertaining to this subject.

And not just read, but ponder; why does God set such firm boundaries with sexual conduct? Why does the subject matter SO much to Him? If God takes sexual matters so seriously, shouldn't we? What does God, in His infinite wisdom, know about the benefits and risks of sexuality that our mortal minds simply can't fathom? And how do we individually need to correct our stance on the matter of sexuality to be in line with His?

What Does the Bible Say About Sexuality?

1 Corinthians 6:18 - Flee from **sexual immorality**. Every other sin a person commits is outside the body, but the sexually immoral person sins against his own body.

1 Thessalonians 4:3-4 - For this is the will of God, your sanctification: that you abstain from **sexual immorality**; that each one of you know how to control his own body in holiness and honor...

Matthew 19:4-6 - He answered, "Have you not read that he who created them from the beginning made them male and female, and said, 'Therefore a man shall leave his father and his mother and hold fast to his wife, and the two shall become one flesh'? So they are no longer two but one flesh.

How Should I Conduct Myself Sexually?

The first step to proper sexual conduct is to understand what the Bible defines as proper; what it says about sex inside and outside of marriage, what is permissible and what isn't, in God's eyes. Then we need to take note of what compulsions might implore us to act outside that conduct.

Is there a desperation for intimacy? A desire to be wanted? A need for thrill and adventure? A wound in the past that hasn't fully healed? A craving for physical pleasure?

To be clear, having desires is not a sin; but we have to be very, very circumspect about our behavior and whether we rule our urges or they rule us. This goes for sexuality as well as urges in every dimension of the human experience.

If we are relating to any matter of sexuality in a way that is discordant with God's word, we need to take proper steps—even drastic ones—to return to alignment with God's will.

It's worth noting that sexual immorality is a kind of misconduct we're told to *flee* from (1 Cor. 6:18). This is because what takes place sexually between two people is profound and powerfully binding, and when it takes place outside of healthy contexts, it can absolutely cause harm.

God is not at all surprised that when it comes to matters of sexuality and sexual conduct, there is an almost inherent weakness in mankind. Some sins are even compared to or addressed through sexual euphemism to emphasize their attraction, such as witchcraft and disobedience. God sets very clear, very firm boundaries about sexual behavior that is healthy and good for both parties involved.

The good news is, when approached with respect to God's boundaries and instructions, sex is a wonderful, natural, healthy, and pure experience. It's not something filthy to be avoided, nor should people feel guilty or shameful for being sexual beings.

But like with everything else we are and anything we do, this wonderful gift should be engaged only within the laws God has laid out; this guarantees the ultimate physical, emotional, and spiritual benefits of the act.

TAKE ACTION:

Is there a place in your life where you find yourself tempted into sexual conduct that opposes God's desires and the boundaries He has laid for proper sexual conduct? What steps can you take TODAY to flee that temptation?

39

UNITY

AS A KID, I WAS obsessed with Aesop's Fables. I probably read our little orange book of them cover to cover a hundred times! Among my favorites was *The Bundle of Sticks*, in which a father, fed up with his sons all quarreling, decides to teach them a lesson. He has them try to break a bundle of sticks, which of course they fail at; then he hands them each a separate stick, which they snap easily.

The lesson? *In unity is strength.*

It's no surprise God has always known this and does not keep that truth from us. Way back in Genesis 11, He said of even the evilest of people who were building a tower to Heaven, "Behold, they are one people, and they have all one language, and this is what they begin to do. Now nothing will be withheld from [be impossible for] them that they intend to do."

This, about the terrible acts the wicked sought to do! All because they were of one language and as one people!

Think about that same principle with the followers of Jesus. When we are unified in mission and in voice, we become an unstoppable force sweeping across the world for the good of the Great One who created us.

In his teachings during his time on earth and since, through the inspired writings of many, Jesus made it known the sheer power of unity among his Body—it is what defines us, empowers us, sets us apart, and makes us strong. We are known as his not by what we know, but how we behave in relationship with one another.

Are we putting as much emphasis on the power of unity as God does? Have we highly esteemed the sheer force of being one people, with one heavenly language, working good together for the One who created us? Do we truly fathom the utter importance of being unified in the holy spirit and having peace?

WHAT IS UNITY?

Merriam-Webster Dictionary defines **unity** as "the quality or state of not being multiple; oneness. A condition of harmony."

What a definition! Nothing could be truer of what Jesus wants for his Body and what we are to be with one another; one and harmonious, not multiple. Though our "core beliefs", practices, and understanding of Scripture may be different, we are meant to treat one another with love and respect and to be one in such a way that people see God and Jesus reflected through us.

This, by the way, is in no way elective. Unity of the spirit is not based on how we *feel* about our fellow Christians who are different from us; it's a command from our Lord Jesus about how we are to conduct ourselves as his representatives and as separate members of his Body.

We are to be one and harmonious in a way that moves the Body forward, every part in synchrony, to carry the Gospel to the world.

What Does the Bible Say About Unity?

1 Peter 3:8 - Finally, all of you, have **unity** of mind, sympathy, brotherly love, a tender heart, and a humble mind.

Ephesians 4:1-3 - I therefore, a prisoner for the Lord, urge you to walk in a manner worthy of the calling to which you have been called, with all humility and gentleness, with patience, bearing with one another in love, eager to maintain the **unity** of the Spirit in the bond of peace.

John 17:23 - I in them and you in me, **that they may become perfectly one**, so that the world may know that you sent me and loved them even as you loved me.

How Can I Become A Force for Unity?

The unity we are specifically told to keep is the "unity of the spirit in the bond of peace"—which means to acknowledge the same gift of holy spirit in every Christian and use that as a foundation to have peace in the Body of Christ.

Here are three vital ways to become a force for unity!

1. **Focus on What Unites Us, Not What Divides**

Truth is important. But understand that every Christian you meet—even the ones you contend with—all believe they've got it figured out. Instead of looking for places where you see things differently from your brothers and sisters in Christ, seek the places where you're of one mind and find ways to spread the Gospel from that position of unity.

2. **Devote Your Attention to What's Important**

We can certainly spend all our time on this earth debating who among us has the greater scope of truth, but in the end, will that bring anyone else to Christ? While there's nothing wrong with a healthy conversation about differing viewpoints, what unifies us as a family is the places where we have respect and love—and those places need to be where we devote the majority of our focus!

3. **Lead with Love**

Remember, Jesus said the world would know we were his disciples not by how much we know, but by how we love one another. Operating from the place of *unity in the spirit*—recognizing we all serve the same Lord and thus are all infilled with the same gift of holy spirit—allows us to approach one another with love, the greatest unifier and the nature of our Father God.

TAKE ACTION:

Is there a place in your life where you've chosen division over unity? How can you be a catalyst for unification with others?

DEATH

WHEN I WAS FOURTEEN, I went with some family friends to slaughter chickens. It was my first time partaking of any farm practices, and as a girl who grew up watching *Emergency Vets* on Animal Planet while eating her scrambled eggs, the gore factor didn't bother me much.

But there was a different kind of solemnity to the experience: the closeness of death.

Death is such a controversial topic in the world, but I think it's safe to say that most people become desensitized to it, to some degree, over the course of their lives. This can come through excessive exposure—like in a trauma ward or battle situation—or minimalized exposure, like your average first-world person today. For those who eat meat, the butchering process is largely separate from the consumption. Back at that farm at fourteen was the first time I looked at an animal before it was killed for my consumption; the first time my heart connected that there was death on the other side of that life-giving sustenance.

Honestly, I don't think God ever intended us to be quite as separate from death as we are today. The fact is, death is a part of life, thanks to the Fall of Adam and Eve; it is a part of man's reality, and I don't think God wants us to forget those consequences.

If you look back at the course of history, all the way to Israel, one of the rules for certain sacrifices was to lay hands on the animal that was killed for atonement. There is an element in that of bringing the wages of sin (death) near; one comes face to face in that moment with the price of a life laid down for theirs, their hands on the innocent (the sacrifice) given for the guilty (the one laying on hands).

People have a vast array of reactions to the threat of death. And yes, death is a terrible thing; but by and large, we have lost our perspective on life and death to such an extreme that we tend *toward* extremes—usually of avoidance or invitation—when we're faced with the reality of death.

We need to have a heavenly perspective on life and death. We need a *godly* perspective, so that we hold a balance rather than causing a problem—for ourselves or others—when it comes to the subject of death.

What Is Death?

Merriam-Webster Dictionary defines **death** as "a permanent cessation of all vital functions; the end of life."

There is little more that needs to be said about what death is; most of us have been touched by it at least somewhere in our lives. Yet it's something our very spirit seems to know we weren't created for and wars valiantly against even in the gravest circumstances.

This is why the story of a man seeking immortality is so universal, popping up endlessly in various forms of entertainment...and why so many have actually wasted their lives trying to attain or discover the secret behind it. Shangri-La, the Fountain of Youth, immortal warriors and thousand-year loves...these themes all manifest the loathing of death within us.

No matter your belief in what comes after, death is undeniably the conclusion of *something*; the end of one's time to make an impact on this world and a separation from loved ones until we are all united in the presence of Jesus.

In short, death is an enemy. And one day, Jesus will conquer it.

What Does the Bible Say About Death?

Ecclesiastes 9:5 - For the living know that they will **die**, but the **dead** know nothing, and they have no more reward, for the memory of them is forgotten.

1 Corinthians 15:26 - The last enemy to be destroyed is **death**.

1 Thessalonians 4:13 - But we do not want you to be uninformed, brothers, about those who are **asleep**

[dead], that you may not grieve as others do who have no hope.

How Should I Relate to Death?

As terrible as death is, there are two things to bear in mind: obsessing over it will not add a day to our lives, and dying is not the end of the born-again believer's story. When death comes for us, as it will for all but those who are alive to see Christ's return, the very next thing we'll know is our Lord's face.

So how should we relate to death? By ultimately accepting it is not about us. Instead, take the steps necessary to make sure those who would be most affected by your passing are taken care of, in case the unthinkable should happen; make sure you have a will or plan in place, not for morbidity's sake, but for preparedness. And then get busy living.

Life is simply too precious to waste dwelling on death. Accept that death will come, should the Lord tarry; accept that it's not the end, pray for peace and protection, and turn your thoughts to things that are honorable, righteous, pure, lovely, admirable, full of virtue and worthy of praise (Phil. 4:8).

If thoughts of death or dying plague you, pray against them in the name of Jesus—you don't have to live in that mindset! Death doesn't have to be a shadow stalking you night and day.

God wants us to live fruitful, abundant lives, and being haunted by the thought of death empowers no one. Cast off that shackle by accepting the gift of life in the age to come by the sacrifice of Jesus, and then let your focus be on doing good in this life and your hope in the day when our Savior will at last destroy the enemy, Death, and we will live forever with him!

TAKE ACTION:

If you find yourself dwelling on thoughts of death, avoid sources that feed these thoughts and invest your time instead on those that inspire you regarding the Hope, everlasting life, and the promises of God!

LIFE

I'VE ALWAYS BEEN SMITTEN WITH the ending of the classic movie *Hook*, where Robin William's Peter Pan declares at the culmination of his journey, "To live would be an awfully big adventure."

The truth is, life can be an adventure any time we're willing to make it one; this life has inherent value, and it's up to us to seize it and make the most of it. I firmly believe we make the choice to redeem or squander every moment of the day; we can either use them for what matters or what doesn't. That's not to say we can never sit and relax! But as we plan our days, may we always remember that the hours are precious.

Life is important. Living it matters. Jesus came so that we could have more abundant lives both now and in eternity; that means it *is* possible to make the most of this one, even in a fallen world. We *can* use these dark days for good; we *can* choose to seek the positive; we *can* win souls for Jesus so they, too, experience the more abundant life Jesus offers to all.

Are we making the most of this life, or coasting through it? Do we prioritize an abundant existence, or are we content with living less than what Jesus wants for us? Do we treat life like an adventure or a chore?

What does *God* want us to do with life? Are we doing *that*?

WHAT IS LIFE?

Merriam-Webster Dictionary defines **life** as "the quality that distinguishes a vital and functional being from a dead body; a principle or force that is considered to underlie the distinctive quality of animate beings."

Just as the human spirit knows and constantly rages against death for which we were not inherently designed, life is imprinted deep within us—a mark of our eternal Creator. We yearn not just to live, but to live well. Human beings are capable of doing great and sometimes terrifying things to survive; some even hold so tightly to their own lives, they devalue the lives of others.

This life can also be one of the greatest single sources of distraction as it draws our attention away from what matters *most*—life in the age to come. The constant struggle for the Christian is to hold the proper estimation of life in this world and the one that will follow, to ensure we squander neither; for both are a gift from our Maker.

What Does the Bible Say About Life?

1 Corinthians 15:22 - For as in Adam all die, so also in Christ shall all be made **alive**.

John 11:25 – Jesus said to her, "I am the resurrection and the life. Whoever believes in me, though he die, yet shall he **live**…

Galatians 2:20 - I have been crucified with Christ. It is no longer I who **live**, but Christ who **lives** in me.

And the life I now **live** in the flesh I **live** by faith in the Son of God, who loved me and gave himself for me.

HOW SHOULD I RELATE TO LIFE?

Recognize that this life is temporary. As full of beauty as it can be, as full of wonder and awe and joy, it is still temporary; don't cling so tightly to it or become so obsessed with having the "perfect" one here that you sacrifice the vital importance of the life to come—the one that will last eternally for those saved by the payment of Jesus's blood for their sins.

There are some in Christian circles who swing so far on this pendulum, they firmly believe that to enjoy anything in this life is a sin, even a betrayal to God; however, that's not the case. Jesus came "so [we] can have life, and have *it* abundantly." (John 10:10). This is not just so that people can live fully in the future with everlasting life and spiritual bodies—though ideally, that's where you're headed!—but also, with Jesus as the source of your strength, the living water from which you drink, you can experience an abundance of life *now*. He wants us to live well both now and in eternity, the right way: through him.

So, how should we relate to this life?

Hold it carefully as the precious gift from God it is; but don't cling to it to the detriment of others or your eternal salvation. This life is a vapor, the one to come is without end for those saved by trust in Jesus. So ensure that you're using *this life* to store up treasure for *that one*.

Think of it as a gift, an opportunity to seek joy and serve God in a way that reaps boundless reward in the future and brings more people into the family of God.

Think of life as a gift—and don't let it be wasted!

TAKE ACTION:

Are the things of this life taking your focus away from the things of God? Approach Him in prayer and ask him to help you develop a perspective in line with how He sees life—so that you can indeed have it more abundantly!

HOLINESS

"IF PRACTICE MAKES PERFECT AND nobody's perfect, why practice?"

I used to *cackle* at this quote. Pretty witty, right? And not a bad argument for skipping soccer tryouts and band meet-ups when you're just not feeling it!

But I think a lot of times the same attitude winnows its way into our spiritual lives; like if Jesus died for our sins already, why not indulge a little? Or if we're never going to be perfect or truly *holy* in this broken world, why strive so hard and deny the things our human nature craves?

It's a question worth asking, right? *What's the point of being holy in this life if we can't do it perfectly?*

The thing is, we want so much out of this life that's *already* incomplete. This world, our bodies, even our experience of God are all just a shadow compared to what we were designed for, the reality He's drawing us back toward.

But holy, upright living in this present age lets us catch a clearer glimpse of eternity, the life God always intended and desired for His children. It opens doors to experience God's majesty in ways we will never know if we're indulging in the so-called pleasures of this life; and to not pursue that holiness because it won't be perfected now is like saying we'll never have a bite of cheesecake because we're not going to eat the whole thing.

Holiness is important because it allows us to draw near to God in the dark age, and Him to us. If we are living in unholiness, it becomes so much harder to see God in this life; He is purely holy, after all, and our darkness can veil our view of His light. We blind ourselves to seeing His goodness when we're wallowing in sin.

Yes, we will still make mistakes when we strive for holy living. No, we won't do it totally right. But we will do *better*, and we will see Him clearer when we try.

And anything that allows us to draw nearer to God is a sacrifice worth making, a risk worth taking, and a goal worth striving toward.

WHAT IS HOLINESS?

Merriam-Webster Dictionary defines **holiness** as "the quality or state of being holy; exalted or worthy of complete devotion as one perfect in goodness and righteousness; devoted entirely to the deity or the work of the deity."

In many ways, the subject of holiness or *being holy* has been hijacked thanks to the combined actions of the pious over the centuries and the reactions of those judging them for their behavior. As a result, holiness has come to have almost a negative connotation, as if one should avoid holy behavior or holy thinking or else risk offending others by seeming like they're better than them; for example, a "holier-than-thou" attitude.

However, at its core, holiness is about seeing as God sees and valuing as He values. It's about putting

His opinion before our own or anyone else's and adjusting our lives to walk in His will, no matter how it comes across to others.

At its core, true holiness is relational and strives to mirror itself to the nature of God.

What Does the Bible Say About Holiness?

Hebrews 12:14 - Strive for peace with everyone, and for the **holiness** without which no one will see the Lord.

1 Peter 1:15-16 - But as he who called you is **holy**, you also be **holy** in all your conduct, since it is written, "You shall be holy, for I am **holy**."

1 Thessalonians 4:7 - For God has not called us for impurity, but in **holiness**.

How Can I Become More Holy?

Holiness is the very nature of God; that's why Scripture calls Him the Holy Spirit, because He is Holy and He is Spirit! Holiness involves loving what God loves, hating what He hates, loving him with all our heart, soul, mind, and strength, and making every attempt to war against the sin nature within us to please Him in our words, thoughts, and deeds.

We cannot become truly holy without conforming to the image, thoughts, and patterns of God rather than of the world.

In order to become holier—to even start on the path of holiness!—we need to take time to learn and deeply understand the things that matter to God and why they are important. Not only do we want to obey His commandments, but we want to dig deep into comprehending why He made them, so that our mindset as well as our conduct is steeped in the same holiness as our Maker.

If you desire to be holy, desire God's heart; if you seek holiness, seek His will, corporately and personally. Just as Jesus told the rich young ruler to abide by God's laws, so we need to abide by His instructions and write them on the tablet of our heart, so that we don't sin against Him.

And that is how we will truly become *holy*.

TAKE ACTION:

Is there any area of your life where you're finding yourself "satisfied" with trying for less than holiness? Take time to surrender that area to God and ask Him to help you see it through HIS eyes!

SOBRIETY

WHEN I WAS IN MY late teens, I stumbled onto a character description in a book that really stuck with me. Most people born after the 80's probably had to read this book in school, so no surprise if you recognize the line: "But Soda never touches a drop [of alcohol]—he doesn't need to. **He gets drunk on just plain living."**

It is so, so easy to get drunk on this life. Not just to enjoy it, not just stepping into those moments like a perfect Christmas display or a day at an amusement park that you want to remember forever...but actually getting intoxicated on everything this world has to offer, in a way that numbs us to the spiritual battle that's always raging.

Sometimes we do this on purpose. Sometimes it happens accidentally. I think a lot about this because it has happened and even now still drags at me a lot...wanting to get stuck on the things in this world that serve as a distraction.

I hear a lot of Christians ask, when does something become idolatry? When do we know we've strayed too far? I think that's really the indicator: when we're intoxicated by it. When the "thing"—whether it's a substance, an experience, a person, a thing, whatever—becomes so all-consuming that we're willing to numb out to the rest of life and get lost in that thing instead.

It's really easy to get drunk on this life. And one of the Enemy's great achievements has been to narrow down the window of what it means to be a "sober-minded Christian". Many think that description encapsulates anyone who avoids imbibing substances to excess, but the truth is we can lose our mental sobriety without ever touching a drop of drink or a drug.

God doesn't call us to just be *physically* sober; He calls us to be *mentally* sober, to stay watchful and clear-headed. When we take deeper inventory of our personal lives, just how many things intoxicate us, taking our focus off the watch we've been called to and the spiritual realities around us, where our attention truly belongs?

WHAT IS SOBRIETY?

Merriam-Webster Dictionary defines **sobriety** as "the quality or state of being sober; marked by sedate or gravely or earnestly thoughtful character or demeanor."

Sobriety is about a lot more than just not getting drunk, high, or intoxicated on any substance; it's a state of readiness and preparedness where we allow *nothing* to interfere with our ability to move and act the moment we are prompted either by circumstances or by the voice of God.

Sobriety doesn't mean we never have fun or enjoy ourselves, but it means we don't let having fun, numbing out, or any kind of pleasure or distraction take precedence over watchfulness.

This is also crucial because the Adversary will look for any lapse in judgement or preparedness to attack us; and if we allow ourselves to be intoxicated by anything, be it substances or other enticements in this world, there is no doubt our enemy will take advantage of that to manipulate, deceive, or harm us.

God wants us to be ready at all times to move on His behalf and be able to use the armor we've been given to protect ourselves. This is why He instructs us, over and over again, on the values of sobriety.

What Does the Bible Say About Sobriety?

1 Peter 5:8 - Be **sober-minded**; be watchful. Your adversary the devil prowls around like a roaring lion, seeking someone to devour.

Ephesians 5:18 - And do not get **drunk** with wine, for that is debauchery, but be filled with the Spirit

1 Timothy 4:5 - As for you, always be **sober-minded**, endure suffering, do the work of an evangelist, fulfill your ministry.

How Can I Become More Sober-Minded?

Discipline and guardianship of one's thoughts, actions, and intake are HUGE factors in remaining sober-minded. As tiring as it can seem, we need to be constantly assessing our thoughts and actions, making sure we are not "checking-out" and making ourselves unavailable to God.

This can often mean denying ourselves what seems to be pleasant or fun and refusing to get caught up in things we know will take us out of commission; but part of dying to self and living for Christ is that we prioritize a life lived in sobriety, refusing to get caught up in those distractions.

In terms of substances, we must always be very clear about how much and *why* we are imbibing. It's true that Paul told Timothy to drink wine to help with his stomach ailments, and indeed, wine can be helpful for things like that! But we can never use one verse to trump dozens of others about a subject. God makes it clear: *don't drink to the point of getting drunk.*

The moment we lose control, we are utterly open to physical and spiritual attack, *and* we run a great risk of making fools of ourselves—and by extension, the One we represent.

We also need to be mindful *why* we are imbibing substances. Having a drink is fine; drinking for the express purpose of "numbing out" sets a very dangerous precedent that is not encouraged by God. If there are things we are imbibing to escape from or avoid, they need to be taken before God and dealt with, otherwise they present another open flank for the Adversary to exploit.

Sober-mindedness requires we stay focused, put the things of God first even when it makes us unpopular, and always bear in mind that there is a spiritual battle raging around us. We don't subject ourselves to anything that can take us out of the game; we know our limits, we are active to confront problems rather than numbing them, and we are always in a mindset of, "I'm here, God. Send me!"

TAKE ACTION:

Do you find there's an area of life where you tend to be high-strung and reactive rather than sober-minded and calm? Or is there something in your life from which you need to abstain—particularly a substance or habit? Take time this week to bring those things to God in prayer and begin bringing them into submission to Christ!

STILLNESS

BUSY, BUSY, BUSY!

That's the way of life these days, a benchmark of success—the busier you are, clearly, the more successful, well-off, and productive you are! Movement has become *meaning*; in this day and age, it's not uncommon to have a packed schedule from before sunrise to well after sunset.

Somewhere in this crazy busyness, we've lost sight of the value of stillness, both internally and externally. It's practically impossible to live an outward life of constant motion and mayhem without those things creeping inside us; it takes a lot of effort indeed to be internally still when we're externally flying. Yet our world continues to promote a lifestyle of "the busier, the better", insinuating our value and productivity is solely measured on a sliding scale of motion.

Yet stillness is built into us, a part of our God-given nature, one of the many ways we're like Him. God rested, and He commanded the Israelites to do the same. God never wanted for His people to be scurrying around every minute of every day, *even if* they were doing Kingdom-work!

Why not? I think He knows that when we're full of busy, we lose the ability to "Peace, be still..." and we lose touch with His still and quiet voice whispering from His holy spirit to *our* spirit.

Turn off your phone. Take a walk out in nature. Go down by a pond—alone. Step away from all the motion of life for a moment and embrace stillness. It might take a bit of time, maybe even a couple tries, but eventually if you actively pursue stillness, it brings about a sense of peace, a calmness like unruffled waters. This allows us to open our hearts, our ears, our minds more clearly to God's leading; it makes us better able to discern His voice above the noise.

Stillness may be frowned upon in a performance-based society, but it's something God cherishes, a lesson built into the fabric of His creation from fallow fields to seasons to growth patterns and everything in between. All of nature needs times of stillness to regroup in order to flourish again. We are no different at all. And it's time we reclaimed the need and value of stillness in our lives, so that we can learn to listen and walk more closely with Him.

What is Stillness?

Merriam-Webster Dictionary defines **stillness** as "calm, tranquil; free from noise or turbulence."

I think of stillness in the inner person as the difference between calm waters or stormy seas. When we're storming, everything is choppy, dangerous, dark, and deadly. We are like the disciples in the boat on the waves; we can't see very far ahead, and even the familiar face of Jesus may be obscured and terrifying to us.

In contrast, stillness is glass-clear waters. It allows us to see not only around us in every direction, but down into the depths below as well. From a place of stillness, we're better able to ascertain what we're dealing with on all sides. We can see our purpose, our heading, and the face of our Lord clearly. Equipped and ready, we are able to strike out from the stillness to reach our God-given destination.

What Does the Bible Say About Stillness?

Psalm 46:10 - "Be **still**, and know that I am God. I will be exalted among the nations, I will be exalted in the earth!"

Isaiah 40:31 - But they who **wait** for the Lord shall renew their strength; they shall mount up with wings like eagles; they shall run and not be weary; they shall walk and not faint

Exodus 14:14 - The Lord will fight for you; you need only to be **still**.

How Can I Become More Still?

Recognize that stillness is not a state of inactivity; quite the opposite. When our natural urge is to be active in every aspect of our own lives, trying to solve problems with our might and minds, being still requires us to cast all our concerns on God and allow Him to work His wonderous ways.

I have found stillness often starts with prayer; before my Heavenly Father, I acknowledge that a problem is too big for me. I can't fix this on my own! I give it up to God, let it rest in His hands. Many times, this act brings an instant wash of peace over me. I find the harried NEED to solve the matter RIGHT NOW goes away. I enter into a realm of stillness within myself...it often feels like a churning sea in my core goes quiet.

Now I'm thinking more clearly. I'm able to recognize when the emotional storm starts swirling again, when I'm starting to slide back into trying to take control. From a place of stillness, where I become aware of these surges, I'm able to enter back into prayer and actively give the matter up to God. I can say, "No. I am not taking this back on. I am trusting You to handle it and fight for me. I am going to be still and listen for Your voice to tell me how and when to move."

Stillness, I've found, is something we have to fight for, *and* it's a place from which we do some of our most powerful fighting in the spirit. In stillness, we refuse to let the Adversary's fiery darts get us spinning. We refuse to be distracted and dragged into the kind of needless racing thoughts and frenzied, useless activity that blinds us to what God is working. Instead we foster this inner stillness, a kind of peaceful awareness that allows us to be conscious of exactly what God is doing and how He would have us act.

Keys to stillness include: prayer, cognition, calm, trust, and readiness. When we rely on God and strive for these things, we become peaceful; we are still. And from that place of stillness, we are attentive and ready for the voice of God, so that we can be part of the solution, not the problem, in bringing peace to a troubled world.

TAKE ACTION:

When moments of tension or crisis arise this week, make a conscious effort to choose stillness over reactivity. Note how it changes the way you approach and handle stressful situations!

CURSING

I STILL REMEMBER THE FIRST time I ever (intentionally) cursed. It probably seems a little strange that the moment stood out to me, but it was during a pivotal time in my life: my first and only year in public school, after growing up homeschooled (and returning to it the following year).

I was on the bus heading to school and a couple seventh graders were being rowdy—the usual suspects who made the ride miserable for the rest of us. At one point, tired and aggravated, I'd finally had enough. Spinning around in my seat, I said, "Why don't you shut the hell up?"

The moment stands out in my memory not because it made me feel powerful among my peers (it did) or because I was asking for a retort from a kid known for fighting (I was), but because I remember how absolutely *awful* I felt afterward. It wasn't the kind of bad you feel when you think you're going to get in trouble, it was a visceral sense that I'd just crossed a line.

That line evaporated over the course of my sixth-grade year, and by the time I returned to homeschooling all the usual cursewords you hear were a regular part of my vocabulary. I loved how empowered they made me feel, but I never quite got past that squirmy feeling after I spoke them. It wasn't until I reached my adult years and stopped trying to impress people with how mouthy I could be that it finally began to make sense why cursing bothered me.

So, I knew all along God said not to engage in obscene talk, right? But what really struck me was that I was praising Him with the same lips that actively and knowingly broke His rules. No wonder the Bible says this ought not to be so!

Think of all the rules God put in place for the Israelites just so they could stand in His holy presence without being consumed; think of the price Jesus paid with his own blood so we could boldly approach God. Yet we dare spread God's praises while we willfully profane things He calls sacred with the same mouth? We sing to Him with a tongue we don't tame to avoid blaspheming things like anatomy, His name, and the sanctity of sex?

As time goes on, I am confronted again and again by the fact that I have to do better. I have to ask myself, is the "conveying of my emotions" or the "empowerment" I feel at using socially-praised obscene speech really worth it when I know the wedge it drives between me and God?

Have you asked yourself the same?

What is Cursing?

Merriam-Webster Dictionary defines **cursing** as "a profane or obscene oath or word."

There are lots of debates about what really constitutes cursing/swearing, whether God is

REALLY against "cussing" as we know it today, etc. What gives us some clarity is that God doesn't just use "cursing" to refer to kinds of speech we should avoid; He makes it clear that filthy, crude, and obscene talk are all to be avoided.

If we're honest with ourselves, we can pretty easily discern what falls into these categories and should be avoided. The harder part is truly steering clear of them, especially when they are so embedded in our culture, our society, and in our own speech and thought patterns!

What Does the Bible Say About Cursing?

Ephesians 5:4 - Let there be no **filthiness** nor **foolish talk** nor **crude joking**, which are out of place, but instead let there be thanksgiving.

Colossians 3:8 - But now you must put them all away: anger, wrath, malice, slander, and **obscene talk** from your mouth.

James 3:10 - From the same mouth come blessing and **cursing**. My brothers, these things ought not to be so.

How Can I Guard Myself Against Cursing?

Because obscene, slanderous speech and cursing are so prevalent in today's society, avoiding them can be one of the hardest of God's commands to adhere to. For one thing, it definitely makes us seem weird; for another, avoiding it or calling it out can be incredibly difficult. Here are three keys that I've found have really helped me pivot both my mind and mouth when it comes to clean speech:

1. Be mindful of what goes in; the more we hear certain words or phrases, the more embedded in our minds they become. I've personally found that if I subject myself to lot of movies, books, social media content, or TV shows that use God's name in vain, those phrases will pop up in my head—and they make me feel absolutely horrible every time I think them. Try to avoid intake of media that's inundated with what God says is wrong (this goes not just for cursing, but any kind of unwholesome thing!).

2. When you catch yourself doing it, repent and correct yourself. This is a super-effective mind-training tool. Sometimes I catch myself saying something I know is disgraceful to God. Rather than letting it slide, if I verbally

apologize and make myself rephrase it, I find I am less likely to say it again.

3. Don't tolerate just to get along. The use of foul language has become a looser and looser standard both in the secular and Christian world as time goes on. Let's face it—we want to talk how we want to talk! But there's no arena where God says it's okay to compromise on His instructions just so we avoid inconvenience. It's okay not to tolerate that kind of talk from yourself—it's also okay to have boundaries where you don't let others curse or speak obscenely in your presence. Be bold to call out when people's conduct makes you uncomfortable; this can bring discomfort of a different sort, but any discomfort we experience confronting a problem in this life is *nothing* compared to the discomfort we will feel if we have to stand before God and try to explain why we tolerated something we knew was wrong.

4. Above all, never forget that a penchant for obscene speech is something Jesus can free you from. Don't be afraid to ask him in prayer for help catching the words before they fall out

of your mouth and retraining your brain so your default is wholesome speech.

TAKE ACTION:

Pay special attention this week to the language you use; if you find yourself defaulting to foul language, take time to repent of it every time it slips out. No matter how many times it happens, don't give up! Keep repenting and keep renewing your speech!

SERVICE

SUCH WISDOM GOD HAD IN making His Church, the Body of His Son, Jesus! There are those who teach and preach and study Scripture for hours, and there are those who set up chairs and bring coffee and make sure everyone has food and gets up to stretch every 15 minutes.

God makes it abundantly clear in His Word that the gifts which keep people out of the spotlight and behind the scenes, keeping things running, are not to be any less esteemed than those at the forefront; this is clear evidence God esteems the place of a servant as highly as any evangelist, pastor, or teacher (we're all called to be servants anyhow!).

In fact, it is often the case that the Church's acts of service bring a clear and distinct witness even to those who are tired of *hearing* about the Gospel and want to see it in action instead.

So if you feel called to a position of serving others, don't sell yourself or your gift short; it is of God, it is mighty and powerful, and its purpose is incredible.

Let's not be afraid to serve wholeheartedly, bringing great witness to God by how we uplift and attend to His precious Church and the world around us!

After all, mankind was made to tend the Garden...and there is plenty of work still to be done.

WHAT IS SERVICE?

Merriam-Webster Dictionary defines **serving** as "to be of use; to be favorable, opportune, or convenient; to be worthy of reliance or trust."

Each of these is a facet to the service God needs from us. Service should be others-oriented and intent on their well-being, not about puffing ourselves up or looking good because we're so helpful.

Our offerings of service should indeed be favorable, opportune, and convenient; we should be offering help not just when it's "a good time" for us, but whenever we see a need we can and should meet!

And we absolutely want to be worthy of reliance and trust; not just to those who we serve, but to the One who gives the gifts by which we serve!

What Does the Bible Say About Service?

1 Peter 4:10 - As each has received a gift, use it to **serve** one another, as good stewards of God's varied grace.

Galatians 5:13 - For you were called to freedom, brothers. Only do not use your freedom as an opportunity for the flesh, but through love **serve** one another.

Romans 12:6-7 - Having gifts that differ according to the grace given to us, let us use them: if prophecy, in proportion to our faith; if **service, in our serving**; the one who teaches, in his teaching;

How Can I Become a Better Servant?

One of the greatest aspects of living a life of service is dying to self. We cannot serve both others and our own self-interests. Jesus demonstrated this beautifully in the way he humbled himself to wash his disciples' feet—an act that many in the ancient world refused to do for one another because it placed them so "low." Yet Jesus demonstrated the servant's heart of placing his own wants and reputation beneath the loving act of service.

In order to be service-oriented, we have to get out of our own way and be willing to love and listen extravagantly. We have to put the needs of others before ourselves; we have to be willing to live without accolades, without the best seats at the table, without the praise and recognition that often comes with a position of high authority.

We have to "go low to go high" – in other words, be willing to be the ones working behind the scenes to ensure everything goes according to God's plan, even if it means nothing happens to shine the spotlight on us.

Servitude can be a demanding lifestyle. But it is never thankless. After all, aren't we all striving for the same words when we stand face to face with God? "Well done, good and faithful <u>servant</u>."

TAKE ACTION:

Take a look at the people around you in your day to day life. How can you be of service to someone today?

LEADERSHIP

THE NOTION OF LEADERSHIP FASCINATES the human psyche. We eagerly tune in to the royal weddings of foreign countries, dive deep into histories of kings and queens, feverishly study the foundation of our own governments, and gravitate often toward books, movies, and other forms of media that feature heroes rising into some role of leadership.

I think it's built into us, this desire to find and follow a righteous leader; it's stamped into our hearts and minds as God's own creation, made to follow Him and His Son.

Yet so many will never find a leader worth following in this life; the concept of ruling or leading in power, as a construct forged by human hands, often attracts the wrong kind of people. And even those who enter into leadership with the best intentions and purest hearts many times don't remain that way.

We see that in the world around us; we see it in fiction; and we see it scripturally, with men like Saul, Solomon, and several kings of Judah and Israel, who began their reigns in humility to God only to become more interested in serving their own desires and agendas as time went on.

Leadership is no cakewalk—for the ones in power to remain pure, and for the people under their leadership to help keep them accountable. This is why God urges us to pray for those in power and authority—because their actions have a direct effect on the people they lead.

But in addition to prayer, we must ask ourselves: are we holding our leaders as accountable as we should? Do we view them in a healthy way? Do we see paladins in ivory towers set to make our lives and world better? Do we consider them servants of the people or our betters sent to pave the way for us? Are we right in our view of what leadership is and should be? Is it a God-view, or have we slowly fallen prey to the construct of human hands that invariably places leaders on a pedestal?

And for those of us who *are* in leadership positions—do we lead the way Jesus commanded? Do we model the servant-leader to the world? Or do we fall prey to the same system of title and power?

Where are we leading? Where are *we* being led?

What is Leadership?

Merriam-Webster Dictionary defines **leadership** as "the office or position of a leader; a person who has commanding authority or influence."

While leadership is often looked at as one in power marching along while others follow, telling them what to do and when and how to do it, the biblical model of leadership as laid out in the Epistles and commanded of saints is far different. God tells us that we should be "servant-leaders"—that those who are guiding the flock would also be among them, dirtying hands, doing hard work, washing the feet of their disciples. This is not the common modern structure where we hero-worship the successful ones who have "made it" to the upper echelons where wealth, status, and title are finally achieved; as one Christian minister put it, "Strength is made for service." Leadership is intended to be a position from which people better and better serve their fellow humans.

Leadership requires sacrifice, humility, discipline, intuition, courage, strength, perseverance, trust, and much more. It is not a position for the faint of heart or those who simply think it would look good on their resume. Leaders are the most in the public eye; a leader's behavior as a recognized representative of Christ could make or break both an unbeliever's acceptance of the Gospel and a saint's willingness to continue serving in the Body.

This is just a part of the reason God calls leaders within the Church to such a high standard. For many, it is truly a matter of life or death.

What Does the Bible Say About Leadership?

Titus 1:7 - For an **overseer**, as God's steward, must be above reproach.

Hebrews 13:7 - Remember your **leaders**, those who spoke to you the word of God. Consider the outcome of their way of life, and imitate their faith.

Romans 12:8 - The one who exhorts, in his exhortation; the one who contributes, in generosity; the one who **leads**, with zeal; the one who does acts of mercy, with cheerfulness

How Can I Be a Leader?

Scripturally, we lead by serving. In fact, the act of service is a huge part of why Jesus was sent. This model was as foreign to the world at Jesus's time as it can be to ours, because it contradicts the prevalent secular view of leaders as the savvy and singular elites.

If you have a vision for leadership, here are some important steps to take:

1. **Examine Yourself.** Make sure your desire for leadership is pure and in line with God's purposes. Leadership coveted for the sake of the title, accolades, paycheck, or power is bereft of blessing and doomed to disaster. Sometimes we don't even fully realize that what we want out of a role is impure, but God

knows our innermost workings and can reveal to us the places where our impurities rise to the surface.

2. **Humble Yourself**: Prepare your heart for service, not style. Get ready to get your hands dirty. Leading in the footsteps of Jesus means getting down in the dust with the worst of the worst, embracing the unembraceable, serving in ways that may be privately exhausting and publicly unpopular. Remember, Jesus washed feet and faced persecution right and left. This an indispensable aspect of leadership...we can expect no better from the world when we are leading.

3. **Prepare Yourself**: Scripture warns us that leaders are held to a higher standard; this is true in both this age, ideally, and in the one to come. Besides that, when one is in a position of spiritual leadership, they have an ever-bigger target on their back from the enemy, who of course wants those leading the flock to be distracted. You need to be ready to deflect those fiery darts, ensuring your life and household are above reproach before you step

into a position of leading others in a life of service to Christ.

This can all seem pretty daunting, but know this: leadership is as profoundly rewarding as it is difficult. The Church desperately needs leaders who are pure-hearted, humble, and prepared. If you feel God is calling you to a position of leadership, trust that He already has plans and purposes in place to provide for and protect you. Don't be afraid to step into that calling—like Esther, perhaps you've been called to *your* position of influence for such a time as this!

TAKE ACTION:

Do you have a calling for leadership in your life? If so, what steps can you take today toward moving into, or excelling even more, in this area where God wants you to serve?

TRUTH

IT'S NO SECRET MANKIND HAS a complicated relationship with *truth*.

We want people to give it to us straight, except when truth hurts. And it often does! A lot of times, even when we want truth, we want it told to us in a way that doesn't hurt our feelings or evoke a negative reaction. But what about when truth doesn't pull its punches; what if there's no easy way around what's right? How do we relate to truth when, as the saying goes, "The truth hurts"?

I think this is part of the reason we've created almost a worldwide culture where truth is divided into little segments...you have "your truth" and I have "my truth" and in order to keep anyone from getting cut on sharp edges, we'll just accept that both our truths are equally real and valid.

Yet if we're all arbiters of different truths, aren't we enslaved in a different way? We make ourselves all gods responsible for upholding, proclaiming, and defending our own truth. Without universal truth, we cannot ever be fully set free; we become enslaved to the dance of moving around *my* truth, *your* truth, *his* truth, *her* truth, without any common standard to which humanity can be held.

I can't hold you to my standard and you can't hold me to yours, but of course, we're gonna try; then suddenly we are all walking around shackled to a nebulous concept of what truth truly is and if anyone's truth has more weight than another's and if so, what's the standard of *that*? How do we decide what's the standard, and how do we know that standard is true?

This is why THE TRUTH sets us free; because while truth may not always be easy, while truth may hurt, it is a solid foundation we can stand on. Universal truth remains true regardless of our opinions, emotions, thoughts, or feelings.

Odd as it may seem, it's when we are rooted in truth that we are the freest of all; because within the boundaries of what is true, we can run our race, knowing we are not about to go plummeting into oblivion.

WHAT IS TRUTH?

Merriam-Webster Dictionary defines **truth** as "the body of real things, events, and facts."

I would postulate that there are two kinds of truth: subjective and universal. They are *not* the same, but I think quite often they're treated as if they are.

Subjective truth is the state of mind we're living in. For example, if I say, "Spiders are scary," this is subjectively true for me, but not universally true for everyone—some people love spiders and even have them as pets!

In another example, relationally speaking, one could say, "*I think* John Smith is out to get me." What's true about this is the person really believes this about John; but the universal truth may be that it was all a misunderstanding.

Subjective truth is often rooted in feelings, emotions, perspective, or personal experience.

Universal truth remains steady despite one's subjective opinion.

Notice "truth" is defined as the body of "REAL things, events, facts." As real as the *emotion* or *feeling* may seem—enough to make you cry when a spider walks on you or enough to make you avoid John Smith at a company picnic—the truth can still be that the spider poses no threat, and neither does John.

We have to be careful not to mistake subjective truth (what I feel based on my perception) with universal truth (what is real *despite* what I feel). Because while everyone's subjective truth is real to them, that doesn't make it *universally true*. And we get in murky waters when we mistake one for the other.

WHAT DOES THE BIBLE SAY ABOUT TRUTH?

John 8:32 - And you will know **the truth**, and **the truth** will set you free.

1 John 3:18 - Little children, let us not love in word or talk but in deed and **in truth.**

Ephesians 4:15 - Rather, speaking **the truth** in love, we are to grow up in every way into him who is the head, into Christ...

How Can I Find Deeper Truth?

The #1 way to find Truth is by searching God's Word. Now, I know for some this is a daunting charge – like, where do I even start? Especially if you've been reading the Bible your whole life, it can feel like familiar passages go in one eye and out the other!

One thing I have found helpful is to shake up the style in which I'm reading. I'll read the Gospels, then the Epistles; then I'll reread some of my favorites in a different version, discovering new truths among the pages. When reading the Bible chronologically, I learned so many new details about the timing and how God's story weaves together!

Some other ways to find deeper truth and new revelations:

- Read a commentary alongside the Bible
- Watch/listen to Christian courses on specific subjects (I have personally found a lot of deep content and new truths by listening to *Messenger International's* video courses!)
- Read companion texts by the contemporaries of Scripture to learn more about the culture and life at that time.
- Specifically research the manners and customs of the Bible times (a great resource

for this is "Bible Manners and Customs" by Rev. G.M. Mackie, revised by John Schoenheit).
- Pick a specific word, phrase, or topic and do a study on it, looking deeply into its different uses and appearances in Scripture.

These are just a few ways to mine the deeper truths of Scripture...and to learn more about universal truth!

TAKE ACTION:

Take time this week to ask God to show you deeper truths about Him, His Son, and his wonderful purposes in Scripture—and to dive into researching and gleaning more from His Word!

PARENTHOOD

JULY 24TH, 2020, IS A day I will never forget. Staring at the two telltale lines on a pregnancy test I'd taken partially as a precaution, mostly as a joke to make my husband sweat a little, my stomach dove. My ears started ringing.

This wasn't happening. I wasn't ready to be a mom. But in the blink of an eye, I *was* a mom.

It's impossible to describe all the big and small ways I've seen God's hand in my son's life. Since well before he was born—years before, in fact, when his name came to me in a dream—I've known this boy had a purpose. But it's absolutely daunting to be the one parenting him *in* that purpose.

There is so much he will need to learn. And there's so much *I* need to learn, about how to lead him to meet his Heavenly Father, and how to discipline him in love and compassion, and how to train him in God's way to give him his best chance at life. I look at all the joys and pressures that come with raising a man of God, and I'm swept up in the love for my son that makes all the fretting and worry and uncertainty worthwhile.

I may not ever feel ready, even now that he's been here a while and each day seems to bring new wonders and challenges; but I'm going to do it anyway, because I love him more than I fear failure. I love him more than anything.

And loving him has given me a unique insight into the heart of God; how He can still love me on my bad days, what His discipline truly is, why He persevered with His people and handed out so many second chances and still forebears with us even when we sin and mess up and get turned around.

It took me a while to get it. But I realize now that parenthood is a step into the heart of God we can't be told about...we must experience it. And I know without a shadow of doubt that without Him, I could never properly raise the son He entrusted to me.

Because without the example of the Perfect Father's perfect love, who ever could?

WHAT IS PARENTHOOD?

Merriam-Webster Dictionary defines **parenthood** as "the position, function, or standing of a parent; one that begets or brings forth offspring; a person who brings up and cares for another."

There are lots of varieties to parenthood, each with its own unique set of challenges. There's biological parenthood—mother, father, and the children that come from their union. But there are also stepparents, adoptive parents, foster parents, surrogate parents (where one fills a parental role without any kind of legal responsibility), legal guardians, kinship care (when grandparents raise grandchildren), and more!

God is deeply invested in the family unit and He deeply wants for families to be whole and successful. No matter what variety of parent you are, God's

Word can help you raise and train up wonderful little humans!

What Does the Bible Say About Parenthood?

Proverbs 22:6 - Train up a child in the way he should go; even when he is old he will not depart from it.

Ephesians 6:4 - Fathers, do not provoke your children to anger, but bring them up in the discipline and instruction of the Lord.

Hebrews 12:7 - It is for discipline that you have to endure. God is treating you as sons. For what son is there whom his father does not discipline?

How Can I Be a Good Parent/Guardian?

One of the reasons parenthood is such an important subject to God is because the parent/child relationship in the temporal is meant to mirror the deeper spiritual reality of how God relates to His children—us! That's why the wisdom of Proverbs and other sections of Scripture portray a relationship that is a balance of love and discipline, evoking clear boundary lines of respect and instructing a relationship without unjust provocation, aggravation, contempt, or disinterest from either side.

To be a good parent is to follow God's example; to balance love and discipline, to keep boundaries, to instruct fairly and treat your children, whether young or grown, like fully-formed people made in the image of God.

Accept that you will not always do this perfectly, but never stop trying to be your best; always remember that most children derive their outlook on God from their relationship with their parents, so in parenthood, just as in all things, try your utmost to display godly qualities.

Equally as important: be honest when you make a mistake. Be willing to apologize to other adults and to your children. Show the value of redemption and forgiveness as well as the strength of parenthood. Never forget you are a flawed human raising flawed humans—but lean into God for the strength to raise them well. Seek His wisdom as you train your children, and He will direct your steps.

Always remember that parenthood, like any step of the life journey, is not taken alone; God is with you. He is ready and willing to help. He wants to help you mirror that deeper spiritual reality in a way that blesses you and your children and brings glory and honor to Him; don't be afraid to reach out to Him for guidance and wisdom to become the best parent you can possibly be!

TAKE ACTION:

Are you a parent, or hope to be one? Take time this week to surrender your current and/or future children's lives, their futures, and your walk as a parent to God. Ask Him to lead you into new and better ways of rearing those small humans He's entrusted to you, and/or to support and mentor your grown children. Make the conscious choice to make parenting a you-and-God together thing, not just you alone!

If you aren't a parent, take time to pray for those around you—and say a special prayer for the parental figures in your own life!

MODESTY

DURING MY TEEN YEARS, I really swung the full pendulum on modesty. I went from wearing crewneck t-shirts and baggy pants, to wearing low-cut stylized shirts, short skirts, and knee-high socks to my very-conservative relatives' houses for holidays.

Somewhere in the exodus of all that nonsense, thank goodness, God was able to reach out and gently turn my heart, opening my eyes to a reality I never would've understood on my own in the throes of my teenaged angst and drama: both my judgy crew-neck and edgy sleeveless phases were exactly the same hurt manifesting in different ways: a desperate need to be different and get noticed for it.

Society and the Church often take the issue of modesty too lightly. We look at it as a clothes-only situation, which will be mended once we legislate for people to pull up their pants and raise their necklines. But the truth, I believe, is much more of a heart-issue than an apparel issue.

Immodesty is a manifestation of a need, quite often even of a hurt, that causes deep insecurity; if the hurt is not healed, no amount of wardrobe adjustment will have a lasting impact.

The Church has a unique and important opportunity to treat not just the symptom, but the wound...to look deeper, see clearer, and address what lies behind the physical choice of how a person dresses or behaves.

Our world does not just have a "modesty problem"; it has a string of broken homes, wounded children, boys and girls and men and women desperate for notice of any kind—and this world is all too eager to feed them what seems like positive attention, if they're willing to behave a certain way for it.

We have the power to step into the gap, to minister, to solve not only the problem of immodest behavior, but the pain that so often lurks at its root.

Are we ready to take that step?

What is Modesty?

Merriam-Webster Dictionary defines **modesty** as "propriety in dress, speech, or conduct."

There's also an element of modesty in not thinking too highly of one's talents or abilities, but in keeping with the general terminology of Scripture, we're going to explore the former definition.

While modesty often refers to dress, I propose it's overall about conduct, *including* attire, attitude, behavior, and speech; and that those who are most immodest are often those with the most hurt in their hearts...the ones most desperately in need of Jesus's redeeming love.

What Does the Bible Say About Modesty?

1 Corinthians 6:19-20 - Or do you not know that your body is a temple of the Holy Spirit within you, whom you have from God? You are not your own, for you were bought with a price. So glorify God in your body.

1 Peter 3:3-4 - Do not let your adorning be external— the braiding of hair and the putting on of gold jewelry, or the clothing you wear— but let your adorning be the hidden person of the heart with the imperishable beauty of a gentle and quiet spirit, which in God's sight is very precious.

How Can I Become More Modest?

Modesty is not just a matter of apparel; it's a matter of heart. People in modest attire can be immodest in word and deed. The goal of immodesty, whether it's in behavior or dress, is always about one thing: drawing attention to oneself, usually by shock-value.

That's why immodesty can exist in places where a dress code is required; people are still perfectly capable of being shocking through crude, crass, or unexpected speech or action. And we can be immodest without fully meaning to if we are focused on snagging attention.

The best way to become modest is to not focus on ourselves; to not be desperate for attention, especially the kind that glorifies our outer appearance or ungodly traits. So often, hurt hearts are eager to draw seeking eyes, because we want to feel accepted, included, loved, paid attention to.

But where propriety draws a proper reaction, impropriety will always draw an improper reaction; sure, we may catch eyes, ears, and attention with immodest dress or behavior, but in the long run, will that really feed our souls? Or is that kind of attention from those people going to perpetuate a cycle that leaves us empty, unfulfilled, and seeking MORE attention?

In Christ, we are already enough. We need to lay aside the desperate need for certain individuals, groups, or even the world at large to pay attention to us. If you're attracting those people by immodesty, it's not because they want the true you...it's that you're a novelty to them. You won't always be able to keep up that appearance; eventually, the novelty wears off, and because the attraction was shallow, the relationship is shallow. It won't last.

If instead we lead with a pure and honest heart, and accept that not everyone will appreciate that about us—but that *God appreciates it*, and that's enough—we will begin to surround ourselves with deep relationships and profound encounters. These will have roots and ideals grounded in what is good, and will endure where interactions prompted by immodesty run out of steam.

Modesty serves as a gateway to help protect us from the pieces of this world that just want to use us up until we're empty. By choosing to conduct ourselves in apparel, word, and deed the way God instructs us, we protect our soft parts and make ourselves more readily available for stronger, safer, and better connections.

TAKE ACTION:

In what areas of life do you struggle with immodesty—either in speech, presentation, or conduct? Take time to surrender these areas to God and begin the conscious work of dethroning those places so they are in propriety to God's will.

GIVING

UNIVERSALLY, THERE IS NEVER ANY shortage of causes to give to. In fact, one can begin to feel oversaturated with the sheer number of things that need support, and it becomes a matter of authenticating and choosing from the many what is most worthy or needful of an individual's time, talents, focus, and energy.

As an example, 2020 found more causes than *ever* vying for people's support; society's response to COVID-19 created hardships for many, with food, financial, and other needs abounding. Businesses and individuals alike sought help, while charities and relief groups scrambled to raise funds that would meet those desperate needs.

But 2020 was no isolated incident. Every corner of the world is home to folks in need of the giving of resources, aid, time, prayer, and more.

My encouragement to us all is this: make sure you are giving to a legitimate cause; there are always needs and also always those seeking to take advantage of genuine needs for their own profit. Additionally, if you cannot give money, give however you can! Pray fervently, lend your voice to righteousness, promote godly businesses, offer a listening ear or a crying shoulder, lead people back to Jesus, spread the Gospel by word of mouth and deed!

Giving and serving, even in difficult times, is not just a matter of how wide your wallet can open; it's how far your heart can reach. Giving is an act of worship before our Creator. Give of your time to hear the plight of others, and move however you can, however you feel led by the Lord.

And know that your giving does not go unnoticed in the heavenlies.

WHAT IS GIVING?

Merriam-Webster Dictionary defines **giving** as "to make a present of; to commit to another as a trust or responsibility and usually for an expressed reason."

However, giving goes above and beyond the mere act of imparting a good or resource; it's an act of support and caring, a testament to what the giver values, even an act of worship when one gives from their heart in support of an organization or cause. It reflects what is considered worthy of parting with one's resources for—be it a cause, a fund, or even the immediate wellbeing of another.

Like the saying "Put your money where your mouth is," giving is an action that proves what we truly care about...what we are willing to commit to something/someone in order to aid its/their endurance, growth, or wellbeing.

WHAT DOES THE BIBLE SAY ABOUT GIVING?

2 Corinthians 9:7 - Each one must **give** as he has decided in his heart, not reluctantly or under compulsion, for God loves a cheerful **giver**.

Proverbs 19:17 - Whoever is **generous** to the poor lends to the Lord, and he will repay him for his deed.

Romans 12:13 - **Contribute** to the needs of the saints and seek to show hospitality.

HOW SHOULD I HANDLE MY GIVING?

A couple of big points made about giving in Scripture are that it's something encouraged by God, and that it's something that should be done from the heart, not because someone is pressured or forced to.

The best way to give is a) to a cause you truly believe in and b) within your means. It's important that we don't give to something or someone out of obligation, with a heart of resentment or anger, or under pressure to give beyond what we are able simply because we feel it is expected or even because we want to seem better-off than we are.

There were even occasions in the Bible, such as with Ananias and Sapphira in the Book of Acts, where the actions and heart-motives behind a seemingly generous gift made it an unacceptable offering to God. In contrast, in the Gospels of Mark and Luke we see a widow who gives of what little she has, and Jesus praises her for her generosity and heart. What mattered in these cases wasn't the amount given; it was the heart of the giver.

We, too, want our hearts to be in the right place when we give, so that our giving is a blessing in every possible way. We don't want to be foolish with how much we give—especially as it can lead to contention, doubt, fear, and harm to one's life or family if they are irresponsible with their assets. Heartfelt and wise giving is always the greatest blessing to all involved!

You can also give of your time, energy, service, prayers, or even with the use of things like social media platforms to support and bring attention to a cause you believe in.

Just like with money, these "gifts of service" should not be done under duress or grudgingly, but cheerfully. If you feel you must give out of obligation, it's better that you don't; instead, give out of your cheer and willingness, and this will invite God to bless not only the cause you're giving to, but you as well!

TAKE ACTION:

Is there a cause, need, or even an individual God has placed on your heart to support by giving of your time, prayer, or resources? How can you prioritize that this week?

HOPE

WHAT BETTER PLACE TO END than hope?

The anachronistic medieval comedy-drama *A Knight's Tale* features a scene where the protagonists gather around to help their friend William write a love letter to his sweetheart. Coming to its conclusion, Geoffrey Chaucer claims, "And now, to finish it," looking to blacksmith Kate, who offers, "With hope. Love should end with hope."

I couldn't agree more—which is why I saved this exploration on hope for last.

Sometimes Christians talk about hope like there's only one thing to hope for—*the Hope*, the Ephesians Hope, the one about the next glorious life. But the longer I live, the more I think God wants us to hope for things *now*—to hope for what He wants to give us. For the things that have His fingerprints all over them.

So, what should we hope for in this current age?

Let's hope for reconciliation in broken relationships, for floundering marriages to pull through, for addicts to choose sobriety, for those struggling with infertility to find their two pink lines. For delayed children to walk and talk, for unity between Christians, for good news for the infirm and miraculous healing like in the times of Jesus.

Let's choose to hope for witnessing opportunities and new friendships and more people to call brothers and sisters as uncertain friends decide to follow Jesus. Let's hope for bright days that smell of linen and lemonade, for coffee shop visits and meals shared with our beloved onesl, for conferences and concerts with our fellow believers, and teaching weekends glorifying God together. Let's hope for our children and grandchildren's future and for joy for all the holy ones who call and who *will call* on Jesus's name.

And let's choose to hope for these things because above all, to see the culmination of something desperately hoped for is to catch a glimpse of *The Hope*—what it will be like when we fall into the arms of Jesus, basking in God's light, at last knowing what it is to be home and safe, fully seen and fully loved.

It's a slice of eternity on earth. And I truly hope for that—for us all.

WHAT IS HOPE?

Merriam-Webster Dictionary defines **hope** as "to cherish a desire with anticipation; to want something to happen or be true."

The beautiful thing is that for everything we hope in Christ, we do not merely have to *want* it to be true; it *will* be. Ours is the hope that cherishes a desire with anticipation; what goes hand in hand with our hope is patience, because we can be certain it is coming, but the road from here to there will be difficult.

WHAT DOES THE BIBLE SAY ABOUT HOPE?

Romans 12:12 - Rejoice in **hope**, be patient in tribulation, be constant in prayer.

1 Peter 1:3 - Blessed be the God and Father of our Lord Jesus Christ! According to his great mercy, he has caused us to be born again to a living **hope** through the resurrection of Jesus Christ from the dead...

Hebrews 6:19 - We have this as a sure and steadfast anchor of the soul, a **hope** that enters into the inner place behind the curtain,

How Can I Become More Hopeful?

Quite a bit of hope is rooted in where we place our focus. Obsession with one's current circumstances, with things we fear or can't control, ultimately invites hopelessness and dejection. Conversely, fixing our eyes on good and profitable matters—things that outlast present tribulations, whether it's a short-term future or eternal perspective—uplifts the heart.

Recognize that there will always be things on the near and far horizon that can upset us. These are the waves that threaten to drown us if our gaze is not fixed on the good, true, profitable things God tells us to dwell on. We have to choose not to let our line of vision be consumed with the "what ifs" and "somedays," and instead fill up our eyes with what is beneficial.

This can be a daunting task at even the best of times—and in this present era more so than ever. People are often shamed for not living in the gravity of the present day. But we can appreciate the weight of the present without letting it rob us of hope; in every circumstance, we can remind ourselves and others that nothing in this world will ever be perfect, but Jesus is still King, and he is still coming back. Not only that, but he provides for us causes to hope every day.

Miracles still happen. Hearts can still turn. Love triumphs. The sun rises, the earth turns, and as imperfect as this life is, God has not abandoned us now, nor will He ever. He provides and blesses even as our heavenly future is being prepared for us.

Never despair. Never lose heart. Press into the promises of God and see the things in the near and distant future which inspire hope. Keep your eyes fixed on Jesus, not on the waves.

Choose hope.

TAKE ACTION:

Spend time in prayer to renew your mind this week, casting down hopeless thoughts as soon as you become aware of them and turning your eyes to Jesus instead!

About
R.S. Dugan

R. S. Dugan joined the Spirit & Truth team as a volunteer in 2008 and has since become a staff member assisting with administration, heading up the Writer's Network, and contributing to the content pool with written works of her own, which is her greatest passion.

An Indiana native, wife, and mother, she is excited to share that passion with future generations and with her own, particularly through the written word. In her free time, Renee loves writing novels, spending time with her family and friends, and visiting every small-town coffee shop she can find.

About
Spirit & Truth

SPIRIT & TRUTH is a worldwide, multimedia, multigenerational learning platform helping people become like Christ together through videos, podcasts, articles, blogs, social media networking, a Bible translation and commentary project, a virtual learning center, online and local fellowships, regional and national events, and more. This effort is spearheaded by a team of varying ages from different walks of life and backgrounds, unified around the goal of helping people experience transformative relationships with God, Jesus Christ, themselves, their families, and the Body of Christ.

www.ingramcontent.com/pod-product-compliance
Lightning Source LLC
Chambersburg PA
CBHW030431010526
44118CB00011B/583